RUNESCAPE®

THE OFFICIAL COOKBOOK

RUNESCAPE®

THE OFFICIAL COOKBOOK

By **Jarrett Melendez** and **Sandra Rosner**

TITAN BOOKS

London

An Insight Editions Book

CONTENTS

PUDDINGS

CAKES AND SWEET SNACKS

BREADS

DRINKS

INTRODUCTION

TEMPUS CESSIT!

(Aris gives you a withering scowl)

Okay, now let me see if I have this story straight . . . .

You, the calendar-challenged adventurer you are, agreed to gather ingredients for the Lumbridge chef exactly ten years to the day after we last defeated the Culinaromancer? Yes, I said ten years to the very day; have all those unexpected trips to see Death ruined your ears? It seems like it—and if I may say so, it has also done very little to improve your fashion sense—but I digress.

As you can no doubt tell by the larger-than-average appearance of this room, I have cast another time-dilation spell to fix your mistake. Yes, yours! We can't even blame the Lumbridge chef for summoning the Culinaromancer this time—it seems that some kind of enchanted ink was used on his ancestor's cookbook to make every one of Franizzard van Lumbcook's recipes irresistible. What? You didn't notice that the chef wanted to cook every dish this time? Well, then you're really not going to like this next part.

The Culinaromancer is back, obviously. And he is many things, but he is not a fool. Merely cooking the favourite dish of each Secret Council member at Duke Horacio's table is not going to cut it, oh no, not after the size of this blunder. To break the spell and free the self-proclaimed leaders of Gielinor, you must re-create every single recipe from Chef Lumbcook's book in its original and unenchanted form. Yes, I know you're an adventurer, but with the Lumbridge chef trapped in the spell this time, you'll have to trade your sword and shield for an apron and skewers. What? Of course it makes sense! It follows the simple principles of arcane thermodynamic polarity, which say that to reverse the north-to-south flow of magic, we simply need to—wait, weren't you listening when I explained this the last time? Well, since Sedridor's third principle has nothing to do with boiling water or icing a cake, you'll just have to take a rain check.

The one thing I don't have to tell you is that the fate of the world once again rests in your flour-dusted hands. Some of these components may be in short supply after throwing such a massive feast, so I have noted alchemical alternatives when possible, along with some of my own savvy culinary insights to get you through. You may also notice some faint, shimmering text. IGNORE IT! Though I tried to erase the enchanted ingredients which caused this whole mess, such ink is notoriously persistent.

Why are you still here? Go!

Scour the lands of Gielinor for ingredients—yes, again—and make each dish exactly as it was originally intended to be savoured. Do this correctly, and not only will you free the Secret Council, but we might finally manage to banish the Culinaromancer for good.

Aris

ACHIEVEMENT DIARY

Name _____   Quest Points _____   Combat Level _____   Total Skill Level _____

Starters	_ / 5	Puddings	_ / 2
Soups and Stews	_ / 7	Cakes and Sweet Snacks	_ / 9
Sauces	_ / 3	Breads	_ / 5
Side Dishes	_ / 5	Drinks	_ / 6
Main Courses	_ / 13		

KITCHEN AREA TASKS

Easy

☐ Cook Shrimps without burning them.

☐ Make a recipe without using any machines other than a range, oven, or stove. No mechanised mixers, either!

☐ Make and try the fiery Infernal Sauce on a dish in this book.

☐ Toast and grind your own spices for a dish of your choice.

☐ Play a game of King's Cup—er, Duke's Cup—with friends.

Medium

☐ Use an ingredient you grew yourself in Veggie Mush or Cabbage Garden Pie.

☐ Create your own banana pizza recipe using the ingredients mentioned in the headnote of Pizza, Three Ways.

☐ Make Holy Biscuits with every god symbol on them.

☐ Make all the new Recipe for Disaster quest dishes—Cooked Fishcake, Yellow Spicy Stew, Infernal Sauce, Veggie Mush, Stuffed Snake, Cooked Jubbly, Slop of Compromise, Brûlée Supreme, Cake of Guidance, Dwarven Rock Cake, Batta, and Short Green Guy—and turn to page 135 to receive your reward.

Hard

☐ Make your own puff pastry when you make Fried Onions.

☐ Make all four kinds of Cake in one day.

☐ Create gingerbread goblins and re-create the Battle of Atarisundri using the Festive Gingerbread Gnomes and the goblins! Bonus points for creative use of frosting.

☐ Serve your friends or clan members a banquet worthy of Recipe for Disaster— Cooked Jubbly, Pumpkin, Spinach Roll, Cake, and mugs of Asgarnian Ale, or another equally fancy spread!

☐ Complete the Achievement Task Diary above by making every recipe in this book—NON-enchanted, of course— and post a picture of your completed Achievement Diary on social media. Use the #CulinaromancerDefeated hashtag!

STARTERS

PIRATE PETE

I hope you brought a pestle and mortar with you to this little shindig, because to save Pirate Pete, we're going to have to make some cakes. No, not chocolate cake, or sponge cake, or those darling little tea cakes served for afternoon teatime. Pirate Pete is a man of the sea, so only fishcakes will do to save him from the Culinaromancer's grasp.

As the preparation of fishcakes is quite simple, the secret will be in the ingredients. To make a finger food fit for a sailor who isn't afraid to blackjack his passengers, you must fish up only the freshest cod, then combine it with bread crumbs, giant crab meat, and a few choice blades of kelp from the waters off the coast of Rimmington. (Yes, I know the Falador Massacre was a dark time, but if you don't get our ingredients, that event will look like the Lumbridge Summer Beach Party compared to what the Culinaromancer has planned.)

Seek out Murphy—he's a master of deep-sea diving and can get you to the bottom of the ocean in no time. Just be sure to bring a fishbowl. What? You trusted me on everything else so far. Why would you question me now?

Lemon Dill Crème

118 millilitres (½ cup) crème fraîche

Juice and zest of 1 lemon

1 tablespoon finely chopped dill

Coarse sea/kosher salt

Black pepper

To Serve

Lemon wedges

COOKED FISHCAKE / *Cod Cakes*

Any chef worth their sea salt will tell you that the quality of the ingredients makes or breaks a dish. In all my vast travels, I have yet to find a better fishcake than the ones made in the dockside stalls of the Fishing Guild located north of Ardougne in Hemenster. Here, fresh-caught cod goes from hook to table in mere minutes to fill the stomach with a hearty meal which even years later one cannot forget. Though the recipe is a closely kept guild secret, this is my attempt to re-create the fishcakes known to sailors and pirates the world over.

YIELD: *About 12* | PREP TIME: *20 minutes* | COOK TIME: *30 minutes* | DIFFICULTY: *Novice*

Equipment
25-centimetre-high (10-inch-high) walled frying pan/skillet

Fish
1 bay leaf

1 lemon, cut to 6-millimetre (¼-inch) slices

1 tablespoon coarse sea/kosher salt

450 grams (1 pound) fresh cod fillets (or any other white fish, like haddock)

✦ *Pinch ground kelp*

Assembly
Juice and zest of 1 lemon

½ bunch dill, finely chopped

2 tablespoons mayonnaise

1 tablespoon whole grain mustard

2 large eggs

2 teaspoons coarse sea/kosher salt

½ teaspoon fresh ground black pepper

1 small shallot, minced

1 stalk celery, finely chopped

85 grams (1 cup) bread crumbs

2 tablespoons neutral oil, such as rapeseed/canola or safflower

1. Fill a 25-centimetre (10-inch), high-walled pan with about 3.8 centimetres (1½ inches) of water. Add the bay leaf, lemon slices, and salt to the skillet and bring to a boil over high heat.

2. Add the cod fillets and reduce to a bare simmer. Cook for about 8 minutes, until the fillets are completely opaque all the way through. Transfer the fillets to a medium bowl and set aside. Discard the poaching liquid, but reserve the pan for cooking the cod cakes.

3. Whisk together the lemon juice and zest, dill, mayonnaise, mustard, eggs, salt, and pepper in a small bowl.

4. Break apart the cod fillets into large chunks. Don't worry about crumbling them into small pieces—they'll break apart further as you mix them with the other ingredients. Toss with the shallot, celery, and bread crumbs, then add the mayonnaise mixture. Gently toss until the ingredients are evenly distributed and the bread crumbs are uniformly moistened.

5. Portion the cod cake mixture using a standard ice-cream scoop or ¼-cup measure. Flatten each portion into a 1.25-centimetre-thick (½-inch-thick) patty with your hands, then set aside on a platter.

6. Heat the oil in the reserved skillet over medium-high until the oil is shimmering. Add half the cod cakes to the pan and cook for 4 to 6 minutes, until deep golden brown. Gently flip the cod cakes with a thin spatula and cook for an additional 4 to 6 minutes. Transfer to a clean serving platter, then repeat the cooking process with the remaining cod cakes.

7. Whisk together the crème fraîche, lemon zest and juice, and dill in a small bowl. Season to taste with salt and pepper. Serve the sauce alongside the hot cod cakes with additional lemon wedges.

SPIDER ON STICK / *Crab Cakes on Skewers*

Even the most adventurous dinner guest may find their courage flagging when faced with the infamous Spider on Stick. To make the dish properly, a large jungle spider must be impaled on bamboo skewers and set to roast over an open fire. Though I highly encourage anyone visiting Karamja to indulge in the experience, this tamer version created for the duke's last Hallowe'en bash proved quite a hit.

YIELD: *4 Skewers* | PREP TIME: *5 minutes* | COOK TIME: *30 minutes* | DIFFICULTY: *Novice*

Equipment

25-centimetre (10-inch) frying pan/skillet

450 grams (1 pound) lump crab meat, picked over for shells

2 spring onions/scallions, minced

2 stalks celery, minced

6 ounces (1½ cups) buttery crackers (such as Ritz), finely crushed

2 large eggs

57 grams (¼ cup) mayonnaise

1 teaspoon Old Bay seasoning

1 teaspoon coarse sea/kosher salt

½ teaspoon fresh black pepper

2 tablespoons neutral oil, such as rapeseed/canola or safflower

1 lemon, cut into wedges

4 bamboo skewers

1 delicate spiderweb

1. Toss the crab meat, scallions, celery, and cracker crumbs together in a large bowl until evenly distributed.

2. Beat the eggs, mayonnaise, Old Bay seasoning, salt, and pepper together in a small bowl until smooth. Add to the crab meat mixture, and gently toss together until the ingredients are evenly distributed and the cracker crumbs are uniformly moistened.

3. Divide the crab cake mixture into 12 equal portions, about the size of a golf ball, or about 3 tablespoons each. Flatten each ball between the palms of your hands.

4. Heat the oil in a 25-centimetre (10-inch) skillet over medium-high heat until the oil is shimmering. Add about half the crab cakes to the pan and cook for about 4 to 6 minutes, until deeply golden brown. Gently flip with a thin spatula and cook for an additional 4 to 6 minutes. Transfer to a clean platter, then repeat the cooking process with the remaining crab cakes.

5. Gently push three crab cakes onto a bamboo skewer. Repeat the process with the remaining crab cakes, then serve with lemon wedges.

KARAMBWAN / Grilled Octopus with Pesto

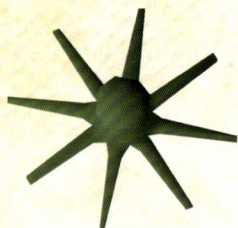

Whenever I need to impress the duke's guests with an opening course, I turn to this rather eye-catching dish. Curling tentacles reaching from a sea of vibrant green work to evoke the tropical island of Karamja from whence this unique cuisine hails. Special care must be taken when preparing karambwan to neutralise its toxins; other cephalopods can be substituted if you have yet to study the preparation methods of the Tai Bwo Wannai tribe.

YIELD: *Serves 4 to 6* | PREP TIME: *90 minutes* | COOK TIME: *10 minutes* | DIFFICULTY: *Intermediate*

Equipment

Large heavy-bottomed pot, food processor, chimney starter

1 whole octopus (about 900 grams or 2 pounds), cleaned

2 ounces Parmesan cheese, grated

35 grams (¼ cup) pine nuts, toasted

2 cloves garlic, peeled and roughly chopped

2 bunches fresh basil leaves (about 72 grams or 3 lightly packed cups)

Juice and zest of 1 lemon

4 tablespoons extra-virgin olive oil, plus 3 tablespoons for tossing

1 teaspoon coarse sea/kosher salt

½ teaspoon black pepper

✦ *1 tablespoon roe*

1. Place the octopus in a large, heavy-bottomed pot. Fill with enough cold water to fully submerge the octopus by 5 centimetres (2 inches). Bring to a boil over high heat, then reduce to a simmer. Cook, covered, until tender, about 45 minutes to 1 hour. The octopus is ready to go once you can pierce the thickest part of a tentacle with a knife with no resistance. Remove from heat and allow the octopus to cool to room temperature in the water.

2. Prepare the pesto while the octopus cools. Add the Parmesan, pine nuts, and garlic cloves to the bowl of a food processor. Pulse to combine, about 1 to 2 minutes. Add the basil leaves and lemon juice and zest, then let the processor run for 1 minute. With the processor running, slowly drizzle in the olive oil, allowing the pesto to process for an additional 30 to 60 seconds after the olive oil has been added. Transfer the pesto to a small bowl, cover, and chill.

3. Trim the tentacles from the octopus. Discard the body, or reserve for another purpose. Transfer the tentacles to a medium bowl and toss with 2 to 3 tablespoons olive oil, along with the salt and pepper, until evenly coated. Set aside—if you're not grilling the octopus immediately, it can be covered and stored in the fridge for up to 3 days.

4. Fill a chimney starter with charcoal, then pack the bottom with newspaper or crumpled brown paper bags. Light the starter and wait for the coals to light all the way through. The coals are ready to use once they are glowing and coated in ash. While the coals light, brush a thin layer of neutral oil on the grill grate (or spray with cooking spray meant for use with a grill). Dump the coals in an even layer on the bottom of your grill. Place the grill grate over the coals, cover the grill, and allow to preheat for about 5 minutes. If using a gas grill, oil the grates, light the burners on high, and allow the grill to preheat for about 5 minutes.

5. Place the prepared octopus on the grill grates and cook uncovered for 3 to 5 minutes, or until lightly charred. Flip the tentacles and cook for an additional 3 to 5 minutes. Transfer to a serving platter, drizzle with pesto, and serve.

FRIED ONIONS / *Caramelised Onion Tart*

Is there any more savoury a smell on a crisp fall evening than the scent of onions baking atop a pillowy square of dough? Typically cooked as a starter, a side for a hearty soup, or as a light lunch, these delicious pastries can also be cut down into smaller shapes to be served as hors d'oeuvres for your next gathering.

When chopping your onions, be sure to save the peels to use in a vegetable stock or produce your own natural yellow dye, like the type made by the upstanding witches of Draynor Village.

YIELD: *Serves 4* | PREP TIME: *90 minutes* | COOK TIME: *30 minutes* | DIFFICULTY: *Novice*

Equipment

Large Dutch oven, 46-by-33-centimetre (18-by-13-inch) baking tray/half-sheet pan

Caramelised Onions

2 tablespoons unsalted butter

2 tablespoons neutral oil, such as rapeseed/canola or safflower

900 grams (2 pounds) brown/yellow onions, peeled, ends trimmed, and sliced to 6-millimetre (¼-inch) slices

2 teaspoons coarse sea/kosher salt

½ teaspoon black pepper

✦ *2 woad leaves*

Assembly

1 sheet frozen puff pastry, thawed according to package instructions

2 large eggs, beaten, plus 1 more for egg wash

60 millilitres (¼ cup) double/heavy cream

2 ounces goat cheese, crumbled

1 tablespoon balsamic vinegar

1 teaspoon fresh thyme leaves, finely chopped

1. Heat the butter and oil together in a large Dutch oven over medium-high heat until the butter starts to melt. Add the onions all at once and season with the salt and pepper. Cover the Dutch oven and allow the onions to sweat for 3 to 5 minutes.

2. Uncover the Dutch oven and continue cooking the onions until softened, about 5 to 7 minutes. Reduce the heat to medium and cook for about 1 hour, stirring occasionally, until deep golden brown and very soft. As the onions cook, their juices may caramelise and harden on the bottom of the Dutch oven—this is called fond. Scrape the fond up with a wooden spoon and stir into the onions. If you have difficulty scraping the fond, splash a tablespoon or two of water into the Dutch oven to loosen it up, repeating as necessary throughout the process. Season with additional salt and pepper, then transfer the caramelised onions to a medium bowl to cool until lukewarm.

3. Heat the oven to 205°C (400°F) and line a half-sheet pan with parchment paper. Add the 2 beaten eggs and cream to the cooled caramelised onions and stir until well mixed.

4. Turn the thawed puff pastry out onto a floured work surface and roll out to a 30-by-23-centimetre (12-by-9-inch) rectangle. Transfer to the parchment-lined baking sheet. Beat the remaining egg together with 1 tablespoon water to make the egg wash. Brush the outer edges with the egg wash to create a 2.5-centimetre (1-inch) border. Fold the edges over to create a 1.25-centimetre-wide (½-inch-wide) lip all around the border, and gently roll with a rolling pin to seal. Brush the border with egg wash.

5. Pour the caramelised onion mixture onto the prepared puff pastry, leaving the border clear of onions. Smooth the onion mixture with a rubber spatula, then bake for 25 to 30 minutes until the pastry border is well puffed and golden brown.

6. Sprinkle the goat cheese over the tart as soon as you remove it from the oven. Allow the cheese to melt for 3 to 5 minutes, then drizzle with balsamic vinegar and sprinkle with the fresh thyme leaves. Slice and serve warm or at room temperature.

SPINACH ROLL / *Savoury Spinach & Cheese Swiss Roll*

One might not imagine that something so humble as a spinach roll could be controversial, and yet mystery continues to surround the edibility of this delicious, leafy wrap. After researching the story of its poisonous nature, I suspect the silly rumour began within the Viyeldi caves which run beneath the Kharazi Jungle. You see, a curse was triggered by a dwarven expedition team which entered the subterranean system in search of pure water, who were then forced to become unthinking protectors of its secrets. Although that event was confirmed by the local Kharazi tribe, the maligning of this pastry's good name seems to come from survivors, who initially attributed their allies' affliction to a batch of spinach rolls purchased from a travelling merchant.

YIELD: *Serves 6* | PREP TIME: *15 minutes* | COOK TIME: *12 minutes* | DIFFICULTY: *Intermediate*

Equipment

23-by-33-centimetre (9-by-13-inch) baking tray/quarter-sheet pan, food processor

Cake

10 ounces frozen spinach, thawed

4 eggs, separated

60 millilitres (¼ cup) neutral oil, such as rapeseed/canola or safflower

½ teaspoon coarse sea/kosher salt

¼ teaspoon black pepper

¼ teaspoon onion powder

¼ teaspoon garlic powder

40 grams (⅓ cup) plain/all-purpose flour

½ teaspoon bicarbonate/baking powder

Pimento Cheese Filling

8 ounces mascarpone cheese

½ small shallot, finely minced

1 tablespoon whole grain mustard

2 teaspoons sweet paprika

½ teaspoon fresh black pepper

4 ounces Red Leicester cheese, shredded

4 ounces aged cheddar, shredded

✦ *1 jug spring water*

1. Heat the oven to 205°C (400°F). Grease a quarter-sheet pan (about 23-by-33 centimetres or 9-by-13 inches) and line with parchment paper.

2. Place the thawed spinach onto a clean kitchen towel. Gather the sides of the towel up to create a bundle, then twist and squeeze the bundle to squeeze out all the excess liquid. Transfer the drained spinach to the bowl of a food processor.

3. Add the egg yolks, oil, salt, pepper, onion powder, and garlic powder to the food processor and pulse until the spinach is very finely chopped and the mixture fairly smooth, about 2 to 4 minutes. Tip the mixture out into a large bowl.

4. Add the flour and baking powder to the spinach mixture and stir until well mixed.

5. Beat the egg whites in a separate bowl with a hand mixer until stiff peaks form. Gently fold the egg whites into the spinach mixture until no large streaks of egg white remain. Pour the mixture into the prepared pan, smoothing with a rubber spatula. Bake for 12 minutes, until set.

6. Loosen the edges of the cake with a thin knife, then turn the cake out onto a clean kitchen towel. Peel the parchment off, then fold the towel over the cake to let cool for just 1 or 2 minutes. The cake should still be warm when you fill it.

7. While the cake bakes, prepare the filling. Add the mascarpone cheese to the bowl of a food processor and pulse until smooth, about 2 minutes. Add the remaining ingredients and pulse until combined, about 1 to 2 minutes.

8. Spread the pimento cheese filling evenly over the still-warm cake, leaving a 1.25-centimetre (½-inch) border clean on one of the short edges. Starting from the clean short edge, carefully roll the cake into a tight spiral. Serve warm or at room temperature, slicing as you go.

SOUPS AND STEWS

EVIL DAVE

Listen, I know you and Evil Dave have a bit of a history. Yes, now that you remind me of all the body swaps and demonic summoning, perhaps that is an understatement. But if we're going to save the universe, you're going to have to overcome your bias against the dark arts, so suck it up!

As with most of Evil Dave's nefarious plots, the secret to success lies within his mother's basement in Edgeville. Yes, I know he calls it the Basement of DOOM, but until he pays the rent, I think we should let his mother Doris decide its name, wouldn't you agree? Glad you see it my way.

Though many other horrors undoubtedly await you in his lair of unwashed socks, your quest is once again quite simple: You merely need to hunt a few hell-rats. Don't worry, they're not evil at all—more like cuddly hamsters which smell a little like rotten eggs. Yes, I suppose that could be considered the slightest bit evil, but who are we to judge? Anyway, be sure to bring a cat with you. They're experts at sniffing out hell-rats which carry the spices you'll need to make Evil Dave's especially evil spicy stew.

And don't worry if your cat looks a bit different for a while after. That's to be expected when hunting hell-rats in Evil Dave's Basement of DOOM, because it is the most EVIL PLACE IN ALL OF GIELINOR EXCEPT FOR MAYBE WHATEVER ROOM ZAMORAK IS CURRENTLY STANDING IN!

Why did I just say that?

YELLOW SPICY STEW / *Thai Yellow Coconut Curry*

Although there is nothing better than a hot bowl of stew on a cold night, an entire season of meat and potatoes is grounds for a culinary revolt. Spice is often a simple way to refresh a boring dish into a new favourite—and depending on your comfort level with either peppers or demonic summonings, a *great* deal of variation can be achieved. This bright yellow curry stew is my personal favourite for its ability to go from mild to dragon fire with a simple adjustment. Just remember that should you choose to use yellow hell-rat spice in place of curry, the results can be quite unpredictable.

YIELD: *Serves 6 to 8* | PREP TIME: *10 minutes* | COOK TIME: *35 minutes* | DIFFICULTY: *Novice*

Equipment
Large Dutch oven

2 cans coconut milk

One 4-ounce jar/can yellow curry paste

2 large brown/yellow onions, peeled and ends trimmed, thinly sliced

4 Yukon gold potatoes (or other waxy varieties, such as Charlotte), peeled and cut into bite-size chunks

900 grams (2 pounds) boneless, skinless chicken thighs, cut into bite-size chunks

2 Thai bird's eye chillis, thinly sliced (optional)

2 teaspoons fish sauce (optional)

Coarse sea/kosher salt (optional)

Cooked white rice, to serve

✦ *Pinch smelling salts*

1. Scoop the layer of coconut fat from both cans of coconut milk and add to a large Dutch oven, along with the curry paste. Heat over medium-high heat until the mixture starts to bubble, then add the onions. Cook for 3 to 5 minutes, until the onions begin to soften.

2. Add the potatoes, along with the remaining liquid from the coconut milk. Bring to a boil, then reduce to a simmer. Cook uncovered for about 20 minutes, until the potatoes are just tender (they should offer a bit of resistance when pierced with a sharp knife or fork).

3. Stir in the chicken and bring back to a boil over high heat. Reduce to a simmer and cook, uncovered, for an additional 10 to 15 minutes, until the chicken is cooked through and tender.

4. Adjust the seasoning and heat level to your taste by adding sliced chillis, fish sauce, or salt. Serve hot over cooked white rice.

STEW / *Waterzooi de Poulet*

Early in my apprenticeship, my teacher imparted these wise words: Be sure to taste the local stew whenever you travel, as you will have tasted the heart of the people. Though most stews begin with the same base of water, potatoes, and meat, it is the small flourishes which transform this humble trio into a hearty masterpiece. The version I'm sharing comes from the famous Falador Farm, which has served this filling, pasture-to-table chicken-based stew to Asgarnia's travellers for generations.

YIELD: *Serves 6 to 8* | PREP TIME: *15 minutes* | COOK TIME: *40 minutes* | DIFFICULTY: *Intermediate*

Equipment
Large Dutch oven

4 tablespoons unsalted butter

2 large carrots, peeled and diced

2 leeks, rinsed well and finely chopped

2 stalks celery, finely chopped

2 large Yukon gold potatoes (or other waxy varieties, such as Charlotte), peeled and diced

3 to 4 boneless, skinless chicken breasts (about 680 to 910 grams or 1½ to 2 pounds)

2 bay leaves

4 sprigs fresh parsley

4 sprigs fresh thyme

4 sprigs fresh tarragon

1.18 litres (5 cups) chicken stock (homemade preferred, or best-quality store-bought)

2 teaspoons coarse sea/kosher salt

236 millilitres (1 cup) double/heavy cream, divided

1 tablespoon corn flour/cornstarch

4 large egg yolks

1 strange potato

1. Heat the butter in a large Dutch oven over medium-high heat until just beginning to foam. Add the carrots, leeks, and celery and cook, stirring frequently, until softened, about 8 to 10 minutes.

2. Add the potatoes, chicken breasts, bay leaves, parsley, thyme, tarragon, chicken stock, and salt. Bring to a boil, then reduce to a gentle simmer. Cook, uncovered, until the chicken is cooked through and the vegetables are tender, about 25 minutes. Transfer the chicken to a bowl and set aside until cool enough to handle.

3. While the chicken cools, whisk 2 tablespoons of the cream with the cornstarch in a medium heatproof bowl until smooth. Add the remaining cream and egg yolks, then whisk until smooth. Transfer about 236 millilitres (1 cup) of the stock to a measuring jug/cup with a spout. While whisking constantly, add the stock to the cream mixture a little bit at a time—just a splash, or you'll risk curdling the eggs. Once 118 millilitres (½ cup) of the stock have been mixed with the cream mixture, pour the remaining 118 millilitres (½ cup) in a slow, steady stream while continuing to whisk.

4. Stir the stock and cream mixture into the soup in the Dutch oven and let cook, stirring frequently, until the stew is slightly thickened, about 5 to 7 minutes. Take care not to let it boil—if you notice the stew start to bubble, reduce the heat. Once the stew has thickened, remove from heat.

5. Shred the chicken with your hands (or two forks if it's still too hot to handle), then stir it back into the stew. Season to taste with additional salt. Serve immediately.

ROCKTAIL SOUP / *Haddock Chowder*

Telling tavern tales of sailing to the Wushanko Isles often leaves a man sitting alone with his lies and an empty tankard. Few captains would dare risk their ship to reach the eastern lands due to the sea monsters, known as kami, which roam its waters. Still, it is not impossible to make the voyage, as was evidenced by a sailor who arrived in Port Sarim some years back (who had a peculiar fondness for large pigs . . .). A few weeks of exploring eventually brought him to Lumbridge, where he asked if I would make this soup from his homeland. Fortunately, I found that the rocktails within the Living Rock Caverns beneath Falador were a perfect match for the fish that roamed the waters of the Wushanko Isles.

YIELD: *Serves 4* | PREP TIME: *10 minutes* | COOK TIME: *40 minutes* | DIFFICULTY: *Novice*

Equipment

2.8-litre (3-quart) saucepan

2 tablespoons unsalted butter

1 large brown/yellow onion, finely chopped

2 teaspoons coarse sea/kosher salt

2 large Yukon gold potatoes (or other waxy varieties, such as Charlotte), peeled and cut into bite-size chunks

2 cans evaporated milk

236 millilitres (1 cup) double/heavy cream

1 bay leaf

450 grams (1 pound) haddock fillets, cut into bite-size chunks

◆ *Heap of bacon*

1. Melt the butter in a 2.8-litre (3-quart) saucepan over medium-high heat. Add the onion and salt and cook, stirring frequently, until the onions are translucent and just barely turning brown on the edges, about 7 to 10 minutes.

2. Add the potatoes, evaporated milk, cream, and bay leaf to the saucepan and bring to a light boil. Reduce to a bare simmer and let cook, stirring occasionally, until the potatoes are tender, about 20 to 25 minutes.

3. Stir in the haddock and bring back to a bare simmer. Cook, stirring occasionally, until the haddock is cooked through and flakes easily, about 5 to 7 minutes more. Season to taste with additional salt, remove and discard the bay leaf, and serve.

GREEN GLOOP SOUP / Ham & Pea Soup

This recipe follows the wise adage: 'Don't knock it until you try it'. To say the cave goblins are a culinarily challenged bunch is an understatement, yet they somehow created this absolute gem of flavour, also known as cave slime soup. The secret is to neutralise the cave slime's defensive poison with a sprinkling of unicorn horn dust before heating it to a full boil.

To make this dish years ago, I was forced to have cave slime shipped by some enterprising goblins south of Hemenster at great expense. Thankfully, the discovery of a similar ecology located beneath the Lumbridge Swamp has since made such extreme efforts unnecessary.

YIELD: *Serves 4 to 6* | PREP TIME: *10 minutes* | COOK TIME: *40 minutes* | DIFFICULTY: *Novice*

Equipment

Large saucepan or Dutch oven, hand/immersion blender or regular blender

2 tablespoons unsalted butter

1 leek, rinsed and finely chopped

2 stalks celery, finely chopped

3 cloves garlic, minced

900 grams (2 pounds) frozen peas

0.95 litre (1 quart) chicken stock

236 millilitres (1 cup) double/heavy cream

2 teaspoons coarse sea/kosher salt

½ teaspoon fresh black pepper

One 8-to-12-ounce gammon/ham steak, diced

✦ *Handful grubs à la mode*

1. Melt the butter in a large saucepan or Dutch oven over medium-high heat. Add the leek and celery and cook, stirring occasionally, until the leeks are translucent, about 7 to 9 minutes. Add the garlic and cook for about 30 seconds longer, stirring constantly, until fragrant.

2. Add the peas, chicken stock, cream, salt, and pepper. Bring to a boil, then reduce to a simmer and cook until the peas are tender, about 5 to 7 minutes. Remove from heat.

3. Use a hand/immersion blender to purée the soup until smooth. You can also use a regular blender to purée the soup in batches, then return the soup to the pot.

4. Bring the soup back to a simmer over medium heat. Add the diced ham and cook until warmed through, about 5 to 7 minutes. Serve immediately.

ARC GUMBO / *Shrimp Gumbo*

A true chef knows that the presentation of a meal is second only to its flavour. As such, a proper bowl of arc gumbo demands the use of a tortle shell bowl for both taste and pizzazz. I know what you're going to say: 'But how can a bowl make any real difference to the taste?' All I can say is try it—you'll understand once you experience the enthrallingly briny essence which can be imparted no other way.

Even if you're unable to secure a tortle shell bowl due to the disrupted trade between Asgarnia and the Wushanko Isles, I would highly encourage you to give this recipe a try. The unique marriage of rich flavours is not to be missed.

YIELD: *Serves 6 to 8* | PREP TIME: *10 minutes* | COOK TIME: *2 hours* | DIFFICULTY: *Intermediate*

Equipment
Large Dutch oven

236 millilitres (1 cup) neutral oil, such as rapeseed/canola or saf-flower, divided

450 grams (1 pound) andouille sausage, sliced into 6-millimetre (¼-inch) coins

120 grams (1 cup) plain/all-purpose flour

1 large brown/yellow onion, finely chopped

2 large green bell peppers, finely chopped

5 stalks celery, finely chopped

8 ounces fresh okra, sliced into 1.25-centimetre (½-inch) coins (or frozen, presliced okra)

2 teaspoons coarse sea/kosher salt

1 teaspoon fresh black pepper

6 cloves garlic, minced

¼ teaspoon cayenne pepper

2 bay leaves

1.4 litres (1½ quarts) seafood stock

450 grams (1 pound) medium shrimp, peeled and deveined

Cooked white rice, to serve

✦ *1 pint smashed rumberries*

1. Heat 1 tablespoon of the oil in a large Dutch oven over medium-high heat. Add the andouille sausage and cook, stirring frequently until well browned, about 5 to 7 minutes. Turn off the heat and transfer the sausage with a slotted spoon to a bowl.

2. Add the remaining oil to the Dutch oven, along with the flour. Cook over medium heat, stirring constantly, until the mixture is roughly the colour of milk chocolate, about 30 to 45 minutes, depending on the strength of your stove. It's important to stir the pot constantly so the roux doesn't burn—if you find that it's darkening too quickly, reduce the heat to medium-low.

3. Immediately add the onion, bell peppers, celery, okra, salt, and pepper as soon as the roux is the proper colour. Cook, stirring frequently, until the vegetables have softened and the onions are just turning translucent, about 10 to 12 minutes longer.

4. Stir in the garlic and cayenne and cook, stirring constantly, until fragrant, about 1 minute longer. Stir in the prepared sausage, bay leaves, and seafood stock. Increase the heat to medium-high to bring to a boil, then reduce to a simmer. Allow to cook, uncovered, for 45 minutes until reduced and thickened.

5. Stir in the shrimp and gently cook until they become completely opaque, about 5 to 8 minutes longer. Remove and discard the bay leaves. Serve immediately over white rice.

If andouille sausage is not available where you live, you can substitute other smoked sausages, kielbasa, or even chorizo! Search for sausage with a rich, smoky flavour.

CHILLI CON CARNE / *Beef & Pork Chilli*

◆►◆◄◆

Much like stew, the flavours of chilli con carne change as one travels the many roads and ports of Gielinor. Aside from the common beef variety, I've had the good fortune to sample chilli con rat, bear, yak, pawya, and wolf!

The version I developed for the duke uses the most common meats available in Lumbridge: beef and pork. About an hour before serving, set some potatoes in the oven (page 41)—there's nothing more satisfying than chilli con carne con potato.

YIELD: *Serves 8* | PREP TIME: *45 minutes* | COOK TIME: *90 minutes* | DIFFICULTY: *Intermediate*

Equipment

Large Dutch oven

900 grams (2 pounds) bone-in beef short ribs, excess fat trimmed

900 grams (2 pounds) pork ribs, excess fat trimmed, cut into 3-rib sections

Coarse sea/kosher salt

Fresh black pepper

3 tablespoons neutral oil, such as rapeseed/canola or safflower

2 large brown/yellow onions, finely chopped

6 cloves garlic, minced

1 tablespoon ground cumin

2 teaspoons ground coriander

1 teaspoon Mexican oregano

1 teaspoon black pepper

½ teaspoon cinnamon

¼ teaspoon ground clove

118 millilitres (½ cup) chicken stock

1 batch Spicy Sauce (page 35)

2 cans dark red kidney beans, drained and well rinsed

2 to 4 tablespoons white maize meal/masa harina

Sour cream, to serve

◆ *2 rankled rabbit cankles*

1. Season the pork and beef ribs liberally with salt and pepper. Heat the oil in a large Dutch oven over medium-high heat until shimmering. Sear the beef and pork ribs in batches, cooking undisturbed for about 5 to 7 minutes on each side, until well seared with a dark brown crust. As each batch finishes, transfer the seared meat to a large plate.

2. Drain the excess rendered fat until only about 2 tablespoons remain in the Dutch oven, then return to the heat. Add the onions to the Dutch oven and cover to let the onions sweat for 2 to 3 minutes—this will force the onions to release their liquid a little faster and create steam, which will help you scrape up the dark brown bits (fond) which have accumulated on the bottom of the pot.

3. Uncover the Dutch oven and scrape up the fond. Cook the onions, stirring occasionally, until they are translucent and beginning to brown on the edges, about 10 minutes. Stir in the garlic, cumin, coriander, oregano, pepper, cinnamon, and clove and cook, stirring constantly, until fragrant, about 30 seconds.

4. Add the chicken stock to the pot and scrape up the fond. Return the meat to the Dutch oven and add the Spicy Sauce. Bring to a boil, then reduce to a simmer. Cover the Dutch oven with the lid slightly ajar and cook, stirring occasionally, for 1 hour, or until the meat is tender enough to slide off the bones.

5. Use a large spoon to remove any excess fat from the surface of the chilli. Transfer the meat to a large bowl and allow to cool until you're able to safely handle it, about 15 minutes. Meanwhile, add the kidney beans to the Dutch oven and bring back to a simmer. Let cook while the meat cools.

6. Once the meat is cool enough to handle, remove and discard the bones and any cartilage. Shred the meat with your bare hands, then return it to the Dutch oven. Season to taste with additional salt if needed.

7. Sprinkle 2 tablespoons masa harina evenly over the chilli. Allow it to hydrate for 1 to 2 minutes, then stir it into the chilli. Bring to a simmer over medium-high heat, stirring frequently until thickened, about 5 minutes. If the chilli is too soupy, add another 1 to 2 tablespoons of masa harina, repeating the same process as before, until thickened to your preferred consistency. Serve hot with dollops of sour cream, if desired.

GOULASH

The right combination of meat, vegetables, and spices can often seem quite magical, even if nothing of the arcane has been used. Still, the most delicious goulash I ever sampled *was* enchanted by a travelling witch with the most darling cauldron who passed through Draynor Village during Hallowe'en. There, I realised the incredible power of food to heighten emotions and, in the right hands, be used as a catalyst for magic.

Although the witch would not share the specific incantations, she was kind enough to offer the food portion of her recipe after a great deal of pleading and grovelling. I suppose I'm quite lucky she didn't turn me into a newt instead.

YIELD: *Serves 8* | PREP TIME: *60 minutes* | COOK TIME: *2 hours* | DIFFICULTY: *Intermediate*

Equipment

Large Dutch oven

1.8 kilograms (4 pounds) bone-in beef short ribs, excess fat trimmed

1 teaspoon coarse sea/kosher salt, plus more for seasoning

Freshly ground black pepper

3 tablespoons neutral oil, such as rapeseed/canola or safflower

3 stalks celery, diced

2 medium brown/yellow onions, diced

2 large red bell peppers, diced

3 tablespoons unsalted butter

6 cloves garlic, minced

2 ounces (½ cup) sweet paprika

30 grams (¼ cup) plain/all-purpose flour

0.95 litre (1 quart) chicken stock

2 bay leaves

450 grams (1 pound) carrots, peeled and cut into bite-size chunks

5 Yukon gold potatoes (or other waxy varieties, such as Charlotte), peeled and cut into bite-size chunks

✦ *1 oxtail*

1. Season the beef ribs liberally with salt and pepper. Heat the oil in a large Dutch oven over medium-high heat until shimmering. Cook the meat in batches, taking care not to overcrowd the Dutch oven, until deeply seared on all sides, about 5 minutes each side. As each batch finishes, transfer the seared meat to a large plate.

2. Drain the excess rendered fat from the Dutch oven until about 2 tablespoons remain, then add the celery, onions, bell peppers, and 1 teaspoon kosher salt. Cook, stirring occasionally, until the onions begin to turn translucent, about 8 to 10 minutes.

3. Add the butter and garlic and cook until the butter is melted and garlic is fragrant, about 1 to 2 minutes. Add the paprika and all-purpose flour and cook, stirring frequently, until the flour and paprika have darkened slightly and the raw flour smell disappears, about 3 to 5 minutes.

4. Return the beef ribs to the Dutch oven, along with the chicken stock and bay leaves. Use a wooden spoon to scrape up any browned bits (fond) from the bottom of the Dutch oven, then bring to a boil. Reduce to a simmer and cover, then allow the goulash to cook until the ribs are just tender, about 60 to 90 minutes.

5. Stir in the carrots and potatoes. Once the goulash begins simmering again, cover and allow to cook for about 25 minutes, or until the potatoes and carrots are tender. By now, the beef ribs should be quite tender and falling off the bone. Gently transfer the beef ribs to a large bowl.

6. Use a pair of tongs to remove the bones from the ribs. Shred the meat with two forks, then return to the Dutch oven. Remove the bay leaves and serve.

SAUCES

OSMAN

I respect that adventuring doesn't require an advanced degree in mathematics, but it seems a reasonable expectation that one such as yourself can count to twelve. Yes, I know you only have ten fingers. No, do not remove your boots in the duke's presence.

Ah, I see your point now, or don't see, as it were, considering that the guest in question is a true master of stealth and intrigue. The vacant chair over there is reserved for none other than Osman, head of the Al Kharid intelligence service and all-around top spy. No, I did not see any evil cats, and the question of whether he may have been lurking in the loo when I cast the time-stop spell is utterly irrelevant! What you should be worried about is how cross Emir Ali Mirza is going to be when his chief advisor is not returned as scheduled.

If you've spent any time out in the Kharidian Desert, then I don't need to explain to you the importance of Osman's work, especially in the lawless city of Pollnivneach where you will find his favourite Infernal Sauce. Seek out the stall of Isma'il, kebab seller extraordinaire, who has unlocked the alchemical secrets to flavourful heat, and be sure to make enough sauce for at least two kebabs. Yes, I said two—sustaining magic of this magnitude works up quite the appetite.

RED HOT SAUCE / *Harissa*

When one mentions the town Pollnivneach, few if any would describe it as a foodie destination. In fact, many might say you unnecessarily risk both your wallet and your life by setting foot within its walls—but those people probably never sampled Isma'il's kebabs covered in his famous red hot sauce.

For such an incredible condiment, the recipe is surprisingly easy. Simply toast and blend the ingredients and you'll never have to beg a bottle from the kebab seller again.

YIELD: *12 ounces8* | **PREP TIME:** *15 minutes* | **COOK TIME:** *15 minutes* | **DIFFICULTY:** *Novice*

Equipment

Large frying pan/skillet, food processor

2 ounces dried guajillo chillis, stemmed and seeded

1 ounce dried pasilla chillis, stemmed and seeded

1 ounce dried Kashmiri chillis, stemmed and seeded

2 to 4 arbol chillis, stemmed and seeded (amount depends on heat preference)

2 teaspoons cumin seeds

1 teaspoon coriander seeds

½ teaspoon caraway seeds

2 tablespoons tomato paste

2 cloves garlic, peeled

4 ounces jarred roasted red peppers, drained

Juice and zest of 1 lemon

1 teaspoon smoked paprika

1 teaspoon coarse sea/kosher salt

118 millilitres (½ cup) extra-virgin olive oil

◆ *1 sq'irkjuice*

1. Toast the chillis in a large dry skillet over medium-high heat, tossing constantly, until fragrant and pliable, 3 to 5 minutes. Transfer to a heatproof bowl and pour enough boiling water over the chillis to completely submerge them. Cover with a plate or cling film/plastic wrap and let sit for 15 minutes to rehydrate.

2. Use the same dry skillet to toast the cumin, coriander, and caraway seeds, tossing constantly over medium-high heat for about 3 minutes, or until fragrant.

3. Add the toasted seeds to the bowl of a food processor, along with the tomato paste and garlic. Pulse until the seeds are broken up and a thick paste forms, about 1 to 3 minutes.

4. Drain the rehydrated chillis well, then add them to the bowl of the food processor, along with the roasted red peppers, lemon juice and zest, smoked paprika, and salt. Pulse to combine and form a thick paste, about 2 to 4 minutes.

5. With the food processor running, slowly pour the olive oil in a gentle, steady stream. Season to taste with additional salt, as needed.

6. Store the harissa in an airtight container. It will keep in the fridge for up to 1 week. Use as a condiment, or to add a punch of spice to marinades, soups and stews, or sauces.

SPICY SAUCE / *Salsa Roja*

No matter if you're cooking for one or one thousand, adaptability is the key to any chef's success in the kitchen. Whether looking to serve a tangy dip for chips, add a bit of bite to eggs, or make a huge cauldron of chilli to feed a crowd for Castle Wars, this smoky, spicy sauce will quickly become your go-to choice.

Although gnome spice can be used instead of paprika to add a regional flair, I developed this version to highlight the local flavours of Misthalin.

YIELD: *1 liter* | PREP TIME: *10 minutes* | COOK TIME: *25 minutes* | DIFFICULTY: *Novice*

Equipment

Large frying pan/skillet, blender

2 ounces dried guajillo chillis, stemmed and seeded

2 ounces dried pasilla chillis, stemmed and seeded

2 ounces dried ancho chillis, stemmed and seeded

½ ounce dried chipotle chillis, stemmed and seeded

4 fresh plum tomatoes, roughly chopped

2 brown/yellow onions, roughly chopped

6 cloves garlic, peeled

2 teaspoons coarse sea/kosher salt

1½ teaspoon ground cumin

1 teaspoon ground coriander

1 teaspoon Mexican oregano

1 teaspoon smoked paprika

Juice and zest of 2 limes

1 gnome spice

1. Toast the chillis in a large dry skillet over medium-high heat, tossing constantly, until pliable and fragrant, about 3 to 5 minutes. Transfer to a heatproof bowl pour enough boiling water over the chillis to completely submerge them. Cover the bowl with a plate or cling film/plastic wrap and let sit for 15 to 20 minutes to rehydrate.

2. Transfer the chillis to a blender, along with 60 millilitres (¼ cup) of the soaking liquid and the rest of the ingredients. Blend until smooth, adding more soaking liquid as needed to reach a thick but still pourable consistency. Season to taste with additional salt as needed.

3. Store the salsa in an airtight container. It will keep in the fridge for up to 1 week. Use as a condiment, a dip for chips, the base for enchiladas, or as the base for Chilli con Carne (page 30).

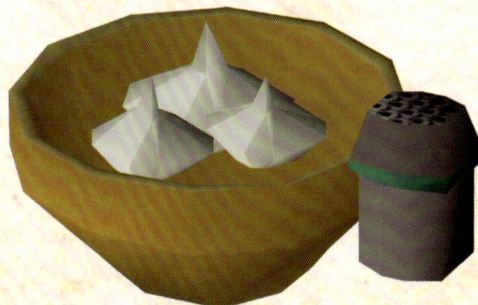

INFERNAL SAUCE / *Habanero Hot Sauce*

Given that the duke of Lumbridge is an important man, there are many who seek his counsel. One such woman spoke of visions which foretold Zamorak's return from within a demonic undercity. Whether or not they proved to be true, I do not know, but she did ask to speak with me before she departed. After confirming I was the chef of Lumbridge, she handed me a hastily scrawled recipe which she claimed to have seen within a kitchen of Zamorak's domain. Though I dared not read the message for many weeks, curiosity finally got the better of me, and what I found was the most diabolically delicious hot sauce ever conceived by man or demon.

YIELD: *12 ounces* | PREP TIME: *10 minutes* | COOK TIME: *20 minutes* | DIFFICULTY: *Novice*

Equipment

Large frying pan/skillet, food processor

2 tablespoons neutral oil, such as rapeseed/canola or safflower

½ medium brown/yellow onion, roughly chopped

2 plum tomatoes, roughly chopped

4 ounces fresh pineapple chunks

4 habanero chillis, stemmed, roughly chopped

2 cloves garlic, peeled

Juice and zest of 2 limes

60 millilitres (¼ cup) white distilled vinegar

1 teaspoon coarse sea/kosher salt

✦ *1 bunch clean torstol*

1. Heat the oil in a large skillet over medium-high heat until shimmering. Add the onions and cook, stirring occasionally, until softened, about 5 minutes.

2. Add the tomatoes, pineapple chunks, chillis, and garlic to the skillet and cook, tossing and stirring occasionally, until softened and fragrant, about 7 to 10 minutes.

3. Transfer the contents of the skillet and any accumulated juices to the bowl of a food processor. Add the lime zest and juice, vinegar, and salt. Pulse until smooth, about 2 to 4 minutes. Season with additional salt to taste, and add additional vinegar or water if the mixture is too thick—it should be a relatively thin, pourable consistency.

4. Store the hot sauce in an airtight container. It will keep in the fridge for up to one week. Serve as a condiment, as dip for chips if you like a lot of heat, or as an ingredient to bring tangy spice to marinades, sauces, soups, and stews.

SIDE DISHES

MARTIN
THE MASTER GARDENER

Take a look around this room.

Yes, I know we're on the clock, but I want you to notice something. Well, now that you mention it, Pirate Pete and Evil Dave could indeed pass as cousins, but that's not important. What I want you to see is the man over there with the green fingers. No, he does not have actual green fingers, but I suppose I deserve that for indulging in idioms.

What's different about Martin, other than his charmingly practical hat, is that he's nothing like the other pompous, self-styled leaders in attendance. He's a gardener, and a darn good one at that. So why, then, was he invited to a meeting of the Secret Council, you ask? The answer is quite literally spread out on the banquet table in front of you.

If it's true that an army marches on their stomachs, then the strength of a kingdom lies directly in the health of its fields and pastures. Though kings tend to get all the glory, you and I know everything would grind to a halt without the hard work and expertise of farmers, which is why freeing Martin is so essential.

To save Draynor Village's favourite horticulturist and preserve the harmony of Gielinor, head to the heartlands to dig up a recipe fit for man and beast. Though Veggie Mush may be humble fare, nothing ensures the happiness of the people like a warm meal.

BAKED POTATO, THREE (OR MORE) WAYS

For a humble tuber which spends its early life underground, the potato is a surprisingly versatile ingredient. Though many ways exist to prepare a baked potato, this method is my personal favourite—the potato will shine when topped with everything from simple butter, cheese, or even mushrooms and onions.

For more adventurous pairings, might I suggest these variations:

Egg Potato: I created this after the duke had a strange dream in which he said he ate a baked potato which tasted like a hearty breakfast. Though it took a few iterations to get the morning spud just right, what I created was a delectable potato with the perfect ratio of vegetables and egg.

Tuna Potato: Perhaps not the best endorsement of its flavour, but my famous Tuna Potato recipe began as a dare. After all, who would think to combine tuna, corn, and a baked potato, other than perhaps some minion of pure evil? Fortunately for Gielinor, I took the bet and created this masterpiece.

Chilli Potato: Though I said I would teach you baked potato three ways, let us not end the fun there. Elsewhere in this book, you'll find the perfect recipe for Chilli con Carne (page 30) which will elevate an already amazing potato into a meat and starch lover's culinary dream. Simply split your potato and spoon a generous portion of chilli right into the middle, and then finish with sour cream and a sprinkle of your favourite cheese.

YIELD: *Serves 4 to 6* | PREP TIME: *10 minutes* | COOK TIME: *90 minutes* | DIFFICULTY: *Novice*

Equipment

23-by-33-centimetre (9-by-13-inch) baking/casserole dish

4 to 6 large white/russet potatoes

1.36 kilograms (3 pounds) coarse sea/kosher salt

4 to 6 tablespoons unsalted butter

Fresh black pepper

✦ *4 bittercap mushrooms*

Egg Potato

4 to 6 tablespoons unsalted butter

4 to 6 small fresh plum tomatoes, core and pulp removed, finely diced

Coarse sea/kosher salt

Ingredients continued on next page

1. Preheat the oven to 220℃ (425°F), with the oven rack set in the middle. Scrub the potatoes under running water and allow to air-dry. Poke holes all over each potato with a fork. Fill a 23-by-33-centimetre (9-by-13-inch) baking dish with a 1.25-centimetre (½-inch) layer of the kosher salt.

2. Arrange the potatoes in the baking dish, leaving some room around each one. Cover with remaining kosher salt, ensuring each potato is completely buried in salt.

3. Bake for 90 minutes, or until the potatoes are easily pierced with a sharp knife, offering no resistance. If the potatoes are still firm, bake for an additional 15 minutes before checking them again.

4. Using tongs or oven mitts, remove the potatoes from the salt, brushing away any excess. Make a deep cut in each potato down the middle and then across it to create an X shape, then push in the ends to split the middle open. Add 1 tablespoon butter to each potato, season with additional salt and fresh black pepper, and serve.

Recipe continued on next page

Black pepper

Fresh thyme, for seasoning

1 large egg

Tuna Potato

8 to 12 ounces (1 to 1½ cups) esquites (page 79)

4 to 8 ounces seared tuna (page 79)

4 to 6 tablespoons unsalted butter

Ancho chilli powder, for topping

Cotija cheese, for topping

Mexican crema, for topping

Chilli Potato

8 to 12 ounces (1 to 1½ cups) Chilli con Carne (page 30)

4 to 6 tablespoons sour cream

4 to 6 tablespoons shredded cheddar cheese

To make the Egg Potato:

Follow steps 1 through 4. For each potato, heat 1 tablespoon butter in a large, nonstick skillet over medium-high heat. Add the plum tomatoes, and season with salt, pepper, and thyme. Reduce the heat to medium-low and cook, tossing occasionally, until softened, about 2 minutes. While the tomatoes cook, beat the eggs in a small bowl vigorously until frothy, about 2 minutes. Add to the pan and cook, stirring constantly, until just barely set. Divide amongst each baked potato and season with additional salt and pepper.

To make the Tuna Potato:

Follow steps 1 through 4. For each potato, heat 2 ounces (¼ cup) leftover esquites and about 1 to 2 ounces leftover seared tuna from Tuna and Corn (page 79) with 1 tablespoon butter in a skillet over medium-high heat, tossing constantly and using a wooden spoon to break up the tuna into small chunks, until heated through. Divide amongst each baked potato, then top with additional ancho chilli powder, crumbled cotija cheese, and a drizzle of crema.

To make the Chilli Potato:

Follow steps 1 through 4, then top each potato with 2 ounces (¼ cup) of hot Chilli con Carne (page 30), 1 tablespoon sour cream, and 1 tablespoon shredded cheddar cheese.

How do you know what types of potatoes to use for different recipes? Russet potatoes, characterised by brown skin, have a thick skin and fluffy flesh which make them perfect for frying and roasting as well as for mashed potatoes and—as you can see here—baked potatoes! Waxy potatoes are dense, making them ideal for soups and stews, as they won't fall apart. White potatoes are considered all-purpose. They're creamy and smooth but hold together when boiled—when in doubt, white potatoes are a safe bet for any recipe.

CABBAGE GARDEN PIE / Cabbage Gratin Pie

With its name commonly used as a substitute for foul language, cabbage gets a bad rap as a stinky, flavourless vegetable, but that couldn't be further from the truth. When paired with other produce such as tomatoes and onions, this odoriferous brassica becomes part of a unique trio of flavour which works beautifully with flaky pastry!

Though garden pies can be adapted to use whatever is in season, one should avoid using the deadly sea cabbages found in the waters around Wushanko and Varlamore.

YIELD: *Serves 6 to 8* | PREP TIME: *45 minutes* | COOK TIME: *1 hour* | DIFFICULTY: *Intermediate*

Equipment

Food processor, large Dutch oven, 23-centimetre (9-inch) pie tin/plate

Piecrust

300 grams (2½ cups) plain/all-purpose flour

16 tablespoons cold unsalted butter, cut into 1.25-centimetre (½-inch) cubes

1 teaspoon coarse sea/kosher salt

78 millilitres (⅓ cup) ice-cold water

Filling

1 medium head cabbage, core removed, roughly chopped

4 tablespoons unsalted butter

1 large brown/yellow onion, finely chopped

6 fresh plum tomatoes, cores and pulp removed, diced

1 teaspoon coarse sea/kosher salt

4 cloves garlic, minced

2 teaspoons fresh thyme

½ teaspoon ground caraway

½ teaspoon fresh black pepper

12 ounces shredded Gouda cheese

1 large egg

1 tablespoon water

Flaky sea salt

◆ *3 Draynor cabbages*

1. Place the flour, butter, and salt in the bowl of a food processor. Pulse until the texture of wet sand, about 2 minutes. Tip the mixture into a large bowl and add the ice water. Mix with a wooden spoon or stiff rubber spatula until moistened through and no dry flour remains. Add an additional 1 to 2 tablespoons of cold water if the dough is too dry. Divide the dough in half, shape into two discs, and tightly wrap with cling film/plastic wrap. Chill for at least 1 hour.

2. Bring a large Dutch oven filled about ¾ of the way with salted water to a boil over high heat. Add the cabbage and return to a boil. Reduce to a rapid simmer and cover. Cook until tender, about 5 minutes, and drain.

3. Return the Dutch oven to the stove. Melt the butter in the Dutch oven over medium-high heat and add the onions. Cook, stirring occasionally, until softened, translucent, and just beginning to brown, about 10 minutes. Add the cabbage and tomatoes to the mix and season with the salt. Cook, stirring occasionally, until most of the juices have cooked off and the cabbage begins to caramelise, about 12 to 15 minutes.

4. Add the garlic, thyme, caraway, and pepper. Cook, stirring frequently, until fragrant, about 1 to 2 minutes longer. Season to taste with additional salt and pepper, if needed, and remove from heat. Transfer the filling to a large bowl and allow to cool to room temperature.

5. Set an oven rack to the lower third of the oven. Preheat the oven to 205°C (400°F). Add the cheese to the filling and toss to combine. Set aside.

Recipe continued on next page

6. Roll one of the discs of pie dough out to a circle about 6 millimetres (¼ inch) thick on a liberally floured work surface. Carefully transfer to a deep 23-centimetre (9-inch) pie plate, allowing the dough to fill the plate with at least 2.5 centimetres (1 inch) of overhang. Transfer to the fridge while you roll out the top crust. Repeat the rolling process with the remaining dough.

7. Transfer the filling to the dough-lined pie plate. Beat the egg and water together in a small bowl. Brush the edges of the dough, then carefully transfer the top crust to the pie plate. Trim the overhang to about 1.25 centimetres (½ inch), then fold the overhang over itself and crimp to seal.

8. Slice two slits in the centre of the top crust to allow steam to escape. Brush the entire surface of the crust with egg wash, and sprinkle with sea salt. Place the pie plate on a baking sheet and bake for 45 minutes to 1 hour, until the crust is deep golden brown and the filling is bubbling. Allow to cool for about 15 to 20 minutes before serving hot, or allow to cool to room temperature and serve.

For a dish like this, finding the freshest ingredients is important! Look for vegetables which are crisp (not soft or soggy) and fragrant, have bright, lively colour, and are firm to the touch. If you have the chance to browse a local farmers market, that can be the best place to get fresh, ready-to-eat vegetables.

VEGGIE MUSH / *Colcannon*

Sometimes as a farmer, you can do everything right and still wind up with evil vegetables. You rotate your crops, sow your fields in the spring, lovingly plant every seed by hand, and yet, come harvesttime, you discover an entire row of evil turnips. Though this is certainly a disappointment, all hope is not lost.

I learnt this recipe from my great-great-grandmother, who used it to survive the great evil vegetable famine of the Fourth Age. To hide the bitterness of an evil turnip, one must combine it with any blend of potato, cabbage, onion, or sweet corn. The result will be a nutritious and filling mash which not only can nourish your family, but can also serve as animal feed for rabbits, chickens, chinchompas, sheep, cows, and yaks.

YIELD: *Serves 6 to 8* | PREP TIME: *10 minutes* | COOK TIME: *30 minutes* | DIFFICULTY: *Novice*

Equipment

Large stockpot, colander, potato masher

Coarse sea/kosher salt

1 head cabbage, cored and roughly chopped

1.13 kilograms (2½ pounds) white/russet potatoes, peeled and roughly chopped

675 grams (1½ pounds) turnips, roots and tops trimmed, peeled and roughly chopped

1 bay leaf

4 sprigs fresh thyme

4 sprigs rosemary

8 tablespoons unsalted butter

118 millilitres (½ cup) double/heavy cream

Fresh black pepper

✦ *3 tablespoons enriched fungal algae*

1. Bring a large stockpot full of heavily salted water to a boil over high heat. Add the cabbage, potatoes, turnips, bay leaf, thyme, and rosemary. Return to a boil, then reduce to a simmer. Cook uncovered for 25 minutes, until the potatoes and turnips are easily pierced with a fork or sharp knife.

2. Drain the pot through a colander and allow the cabbage, potatoes, and turnips to sit and continue draining while you prepare the butter and cream. Remove and discard the herbs.

3. Return the stockpot to the stove. Add the butter and cream to the pot and cook over medium heat until the butter is melted. Return the drained cabbage, potatoes, and turnips to the pot. Mash the vegetables together with a potato masher, tossing with the butter and cream as you go, until combined but still somewhat chunky. Season with salt and pepper to taste. Serve immediately.

PUMPKIN / *Baked Stuffed Pumpkin*

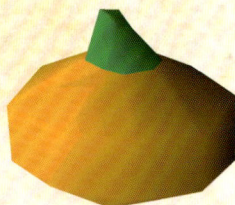

◆ ◆

I once met an adventurer with the strangest travel companion: a baby troll by the name of Pumpkin. As the story goes, the warrior left his bags unattended near the youngling's camp, which allowed the troll to crawl inside and eat one of his rare vegetables. Trolls are named after the first thing they eat, so the little baby now bore the name Pumpkin—a very un-troll-like name. As a result, the adventurer adopted the young troll, and together they sought quests for gold and glory.

I've since had the pleasure of sampling this rare namesake squash firsthand during the Hallowe'en festival. Should you ever be so fortunate as to find your own perfect orange pumpkin, please consider this recipe the ideal preparation.

YIELD: *Serves 4* | PREP TIME: *90 minutes* | COOK TIME: *1 hour* | DIFFICULTY: *Intermediate*

Equipment

Oven-safe wire cooling rack, 46-by-33-centimetre (18-by-13-inch) baking tray/half-sheet pan, large frying pan/skillet

¾ loaf brioche (about 12 ounces), sliced

4 sugar pumpkins or 2 large acorn squashes

2 tablespoons neutral oil, such as rapeseed/canola or safflower

8 ounces sausage meat/raw breakfast sausage (see note)

2 carrots, peeled and finely chopped

1 stalk celery, finely chopped

1 shallot, minced

2 cloves garlic, minced

2 teaspoons fresh thyme leaves, roughly chopped

1 teaspoon coarse sea/kosher salt

½ teaspoon fresh black pepper

50 grams (⅓ cup) dried cherries, roughly chopped

354 millilitres (1½ cups) double/heavy cream

Ingredients continued on next page

1. Preheat the oven to 93.3°C (200°F) with a rack placed in the middle. Set an oven-safe wire cooling rack in a half-sheet pan. Line the wire rack with the slices of brioche and bake until dry and very lightly toasted, about 45 minutes. Remove and let cool, then cut into 1.25-centimetre (½-inch) cubes.

2. Prepare the pumpkins and filling as the bread dries in the oven. If you're using pumpkins, carve a wide circle around the stem (as if carving a tiny jack-o'-lantern) and pull the top off each pumpkin. Set aside. Use a large spoon to scoop the seeds and fibres out of the pumpkins, and discard. Season the inside with salt and pepper. If using acorn squashes, cut them in half and, if needed, trim a thin slice from the uncut sides so they sit flat and level. Remove the seeds and fibres with a spoon and season with salt and pepper. Set aside.

3. Heat the oil in a large skillet over medium-high heat until just shimmering. Add the sausage and cook, breaking apart with a wooden spoon and stirring occasionally, until deep golden brown with some crispy bits, about 10 to 15 minutes. Transfer the meat to a large bowl.

4. Drain excess fat from the skillet until only 2 tablespoons remain. Add the carrots and celery and cook, stirring occasionally, until softened, about 5 to 7 minutes. Add the shallot, garlic, thyme, salt, and pepper, and cook, stirring constantly, until fragrant, about 1 minute longer. Remove from heat and transfer to the bowl with the meat.

Recipe continued on next page

118 millilitres (½ cup) whole milk

4 large eggs

✦ *1 unburnt shrimp*

For the breakfast sausage, Lincolnshire or Cumberland sausages with the skins removed work beautifully for this recipe. They impart a lot of flavour into the dish!

5. Increase the oven temperature to 205°C (400°F) and line a half-sheet pan with foil. Line up the pumpkins or acorn squashes on the pan (if using pumpkins, cover them with the trimmed-off tops) and bake for about 25 minutes, until just barely tender. A fork or sharp knife poked into the flesh should meet with some resistance.

6. While the pumpkins bake, add the prepared bread cubes and dried cherries to the bowl with the sausage and cooked vegetables. Toss to combine. Taste a spoonful of the mixture and add additional salt and pepper if needed.

7. Beat the cream, whole milk, and eggs together in a small bowl until smooth. Add to the stuffing mixture and toss until evenly coated. Let sit, tossing occasionally, until most of the cream-and-egg mixture has been absorbed, about 10 minutes.

8. Remove the precooked pumpkins from the oven. Divide the stuffing evenly amongst them, but do not replace the caps—leave them on the foil-lined baking sheet to continue cooking. Bake for an additional 30 minutes, until the pumpkins are quite tender but still hold their shape and the stuffing is crisp on top. Serve immediately.

FRIED MUSHROOMS / *Sautéed Wild Mushrooms*

Gielinor is home to a rich diversity of life, including an unknown number of mushroom species such as Morchella mushrooms, Mort Myre fungus, stinkshrooms, and sulliusceps. For cooking, however, it is the bittercap mushroom which reigns supreme.

Though look-alikes to the bittercap are rare throughout much of the world, it is highly suggested that inexperienced mushroom hunters rely on a guide when seeking them within the swamps of Morytania. Here, toxic specimens will give off a red spore print and should therefore be discarded.

When cooking bittercaps, take special care not to cook over too high heat. Mushrooms can be quite delicate, but the reward for patience and diligence—perfect, crispy, tender mushrooms—is well worth the effort.

YIELD: *Serves 4 to 6* | PREP TIME: *10 minutes* | COOK TIME: *25 minutes* | DIFFICULTY: *Novice*

Equipment
Large Dutch oven

4 tablespoons unsalted butter, plus more as needed

2 tablespoons extra-virgin olive oil, plus more as needed

450 grams (1 pound) mixed wild mushrooms (maitake, shiitake, oyster, trumpet, chanterelle), roughly chopped or torn, stemmed

2 teaspoon coarse sea/kosher salt

1 teaspoon fresh black pepper

1 shallot, minced

2 cloves garlic, minced

1 tablespoon fresh thyme leaves, roughly chopped

1 tablespoon soy sauce

✦ *1½ caps black mushrooms*

1. Melt the butter and olive oil together in a large Dutch oven over medium-high heat. Add the mushrooms all at once, along with the salt and pepper.

2. Cook, stirring occasionally, until the mushrooms have released all their juices and begin to turn golden brown all over and crisp at the edges, about 15 to 20 minutes. If the pan starts to look dry, add an additional tablespoon of olive oil as needed.

3. Add an additional 1 tablespoon unsalted butter to the Dutch oven, along with the shallot, garlic, and thyme. Cook, stirring constantly, until fragrant, about 1 to 2 minutes longer. Add the soy sauce and toss to combine. Remove from heat. Season to taste with additional salt and pepper as needed. Serve as a side dish with roasted or seared meats, stirred into soups and stews, or as a topping for a baked potato (page 41).

MAIN COURSES

SKRACH UGLOGWEE

By now, you've undoubtedly noticed the giant ogre in the room with an outsized appetite for all things chompy. Unfortunately for us—and by us, I mean you—Skrach Uglogwee has recently developed quite a taste for the finer poultry in life and can only be freed by eating the biggest, juiciest of all chompy birds—the jubbly chompy.

Head to the Feldip Hills and speak with an ogre by the name of Rantz to unlock the ogre secrets of hunting and spit-roasting. Yes, I know there's a range in Lumbridge Castle, and I agree that it is quite nice, but have you ever seen the size of a jubbly in the wild? Let's just say we're all lucky they didn't evolve to become apex predators, or this would be a very different story.

KING AWOWOGEI

Do you see the monkey over there sitting at the table? Don't stare! Primates hate that sort of thing, and primate monarchs even more. Did you take note of King Awowogei's pendant? Yes, very astute of you; it is indeed an M'speak amulet, which allows for communication between our two species. I don't suppose there's any chance you have one of those in that bag of junk you carry around? A pity, then, because it would have made getting the King's favourite dish a great deal easier.

First, you must seek the three wise monkeys of the Temple of Marimbo: Iwazaru, Kikazaru, and Mizaru. Cursed by a priest short on reagents, the trio are the only ones besides Awowogei himself to know the recipe for roasted Stuffed Snake, but getting the information out of them is going to test your skills of subterfuge.

Well, of course you're going to have to convince them you're a primate—the island isn't called Ape Atoll for nothing! Simply tell them the King wants his favourite dish for his birthday, and I bet they'll be falling over themselves to help you get the bananas, nuts, and snake we need. Remember, you can't simply use any old garden-variety banana for royalty. Not unless you want to be cursed, anyway.

UGTHANKI KEBAB / *Spiced Lamb Kebab*

To make a true Ugthanki Kebab, one must travel south of Shantay Pass and survive the rigours of the Kharidian Desert. Here, running out of water is a matter of life and death, but the reward of tasting the seared and succulent meat of the ugthanki camel is, for many, well worth the risk. If a desert trek is not in your near future, however, lamb offers a very good approximation.

Should you choose to hunt your own ugthanki, be aware that they are highly aggressive—and known to spit a substance better left to the imagination.

YIELD: *8 skewers* | PREP TIME: *35 minutes* | COOK TIME: *8 minutes* | DIFFICULTY: *Novice*

Equipment

Chimney starter, BBQ or grill, 8 bamboo skewers (soaked in water for at least 1 hour)

450 grams (1 pound) ground lamb

2 cloves garlic, finely minced

1 small shallot, finely minced

2 tablespoons coriander/cilantro leaves and fine stems, finely chopped

1 teaspoon coarse sea/kosher salt

1 teaspoon ground cumin

1 teaspoon ground coriander

½ teaspoon fresh black pepper

◆ *1 allotment-grown tomato and onion*

Harissa Yoghurt

118 millilitres (½ cup) plain Greek yoghurt

1 tablespoon Red Hot Sauce (page 34)

Juice of 1 lemon

To Serve

Shredded iceberg lettuce

Pitta Bread (page 113)

1. Fill a chimney starter with charcoal, then pack the bottom with newspaper or crumpled brown paper bags. Light the starter and wait for the coals to light all the way through. The coals are ready to use once they are glowing and coated in ash. While the coals light, brush a thin layer of neutral oil on the grill grate (or spray with cooking spray meant for use with a grill). Dump the coals in an even layer on the bottom of your grill. Place the grill grate over the coals, cover the grill, and allow to preheat for about 5 minutes. If using a gas grill, oil the grates, light the burners on high, and allow the grill to preheat for about 5 minutes.

2. While the charcoals light, prepare the kebabs. Place the lamb in a large bowl. Break apart with your hands and scatter into an even layer. Scatter the garlic, shallot, coriander/cilantro, salt, cumin, ground coriander, and pepper over the lamb. Toss with your hands to combine and evenly distribute the ingredients.

3. Divide the lamb mixture into eight equal portions. Form the portions into long logs on each skewer, compressing them so they adhere to the skewers. Set aside.

4. Whisk together the Greek yoghurt, Red Hot Sauce, and lemon juice. Season with additional salt, if needed. Set aside.

5. Cook the kebabs on the grill until lightly charred, about 3 to 5 minutes. Flip, using tongs if necessary, and cook for an additional 3 minutes. Serve on a bed of shredded iceberg lettuce with the Pitta Bread and Harissa Yoghurt. For the best experience, open up one side of the Pitta Bread, fill with iceberg lettuce and the kebab meat, and drizzle with the Harissa Yoghurt.

COOKED OOMLIE WRAP / *Pollo Pibil*

◄ ◆ ►

Some seasons back, I accepted a most gracious invitation from Karamja's foremost chef to spend several weeks in Shilo Village as part of a culinary exchange. There, I fell in love with the delectable taste of the native oomlie bird and a positively mesmerising marinade made from citrus and local seeds.

Although oomlies and chompies are often interchangeable in many recipes, the oomlie's distinct succulence and flavour particularly shine here through use of a leafy envelope to maintain its unrivaled juiciness. Palm leaves are traditionally used by the Kharazi tribes where the oomlie roams, but I've found that banana leaves are often easier to source and provide the same protective quality.

YIELD: *Serves 8* | PREP TIME: *10 minutes, plus 4 to 12 hours marinating time* | COOK TIME: *80 minutes* | DIFFICULTY: *Novice*

Equipment

Blender, 46-by-33-centimetre (18-by-13-inch) baking tray/half-sheet pan, butcher's twine, meat thermometer

Marinade

2 tablespoons achiote paste

6 cloves garlic

2 large brown/yellow onions, sliced, divided

118 millilitres (½ cup) fresh squeezed orange juice

60 millilitres (¼ cup) lime juice

60 millilitres (¼ cup) lemon juice

1 tablespoon coarse sea/kosher salt

2 teaspoons ground cumin

1 teaspoon ground coriander

1 teaspoon Mexican oregano

1 teaspoon fresh black pepper

½ teaspoon ground cinnamon

¼ teaspoon ground clove

Ingredients continued on next page

1. Place the achiote paste, garlic, ½ the sliced onions, orange juice, lime juice, lemon juice, salt, cumin, ground coriander, Mexican oregano, pepper, cinnamon, and clove in a blender. Blend on high until smooth, about 2 minutes.

2. Place the chicken breasts in a plastic bag with a zip top and pour in the prepared marinade. Zip the bag most of the way shut, then squeeze as much of the air out as possible before sealing it the rest of the way. Place in a bowl in case the bag leaks, then chill for a minimum of 4 hours (up to 12 hours).

3. Preheat the oven to 230°C (450°F) and place one rack in the centre position and one in the top position. Line a half-sheet pan with the banana leaves in a cross shape. Line the centre of the top leaf with the sliced tomatoes and remaining sliced onions. Place the marinated chicken on top of the onions and tomatoes, along with the marinade.

4. Wrap the banana leaves in a tight bundle, securing the wrap with butcher's twine. If desired, wrap the entire bundle in aluminium foil (you can use just the foil if you can't source banana leaves).

5. Roast the chicken on the middle rack for about 1 hour, or until an instant-read thermometer registers 65°C (150°F) when inserted into the thickest part of the chicken breasts (poke the thermometer through the packet, rather than unwrapping the entire thing). Once the internal temperature hits 65°C (150°F), remove the chicken from the oven and cut a large square in the top of the packet to reveal the chicken.

Recipe continued on next page

Pollo Pibil

4 skin-on, bone-in chicken breasts, about 1.8 to 2.7 kilograms (4 to 6 pounds)

Two 30-to-60-centimetre (12-by-24-inch) fresh banana leaves

4 fresh plum tomatoes, sliced

To Serve

Warm corn tortillas

Mexican crema

Cotija cheese

Infernal Sauce (page 36)

✦ *22 palm leaves*

6. Increase the oven temperature to 260℃ (500°F) and return the chicken to the oven, but on the top rack this time, and allow to roast for an additional 20 minutes, or until the internal temperature reaches 74℃ (165°F) and the chicken has browned on top.

7. Remove the chicken from the oven and serve with warm tortillas, Mexican crema, cotija cheese, and Infernal Sauce.

FISH / *Whole Grilled Red Snapper*

For those not from a coastal climate, preparing fish can often seem a daunting task. Fortunately, once you learn the simple process of cleaning one type of fish, that skill tends to carry over to most others, as do their methods of cooking. For this recipe, I use a fish local to Lumbridge, but you should feel free to substitute any white fish which you have the skill and bait to catch. After all, nothing tastes quite as good as food grown or caught yourself.

YIELD: *Serves 4* | PREP TIME: *35 minutes* | COOK TIME: *20 minutes* | DIFFICULTY: *Intermediate*

Equipment

Chimney starter

4 whole red snapper, cleaned, scaled, and patted dry, about 675 grams (1½ pounds) each

2 tablespoons neutral oil, such as rapeseed/canola or safflower

Coarse sea/kosher salt

Fresh black pepper

1 lemon, sliced into 6-millimetre (¼-inch) slices

1 bunch fresh coriander/cilantro

1 bunch dill

Lemon wedges

✦ *3 rubium ore*

1. Fill a chimney starter with charcoal, then pack the bottom with newspaper or crumpled brown paper bags. Light the starter and wait for the coals to light all the way through. The coals are ready to use once they are glowing and coated in ash. While the coals light, brush a thin layer of neutral oil on the grill grate (or spray with cooking spray meant for use with a grill). Dump the coals in an even layer on the bottom of your grill. Place the grill grate over the coals, cover the grill, and allow to preheat for about 5 minutes. If using a gas grill, oil the grates, light the burners on high, and allow the grill to preheat for about 5 minutes.

2. While the charcoal lights, brush the red snapper inside and out with oil. Season all over, inside and out, with salt and pepper. Place 2 or 3 lemon slices in the cavity of each fish.

3. Divide the herb bunches into 4 equal bundles and stuff into the cavity of each fish. Grill the fish for 7 to 10 minutes on each side, until the skin is charred, and the flesh is opaque and flaky but still moist. Serve with additional lemon wedges.

To cook the snapper in an oven, prepare the fish as directed and roast at 220°C (425°F) on a parchment-lined half-sheet pan for 30 to 40 minutes, until the skin is crisp and the flesh is opaque, flaky, and still moist.

SHRIMPS / *Blackened Shrimp Tacos*

Though thoughts of summertime often focus on the season's cornucopia of produce, my mind goes to the first dish I learnt to cook: fire-blackened shrimp. I hold many fond memories of building fires along the Lumbridge riverbank to roast (and occasionally burn) shrimp skewers with friends and family. This recipe uses the extra shrimp from such simple communal fare and turns it into a meal worthy of any table or festival.

YIELD: *Serves 4* | PREP TIME: *35 minutes* | COOK TIME: *10 minutes* | DIFFICULTY: *Novice*

Equipment

Chimney starter, BBQ or grill, perforated grill pan or griddle

Blackened Shrimp

450 grams (1 pound) medium shrimp, peeled and deveined

1 teaspoon smoked paprika

1 teaspoon onion powder

½ teaspoon coarse sea/kosher salt

½ teaspoon ground cumin

½ teaspoon garlic powder

½ teaspoon dried thyme

¼ teaspoon dried oregano

3 tablespoons neutral oil, such as rapeseed/canola or safflower

Juice and zest of 2 limes

Slaw

¼ head red cabbage, shredded

¼ head green cabbage, shredded

118 millilitres (½ cup) Mexican crema

Juice of 2 limes

½ teaspoon coarse sea/kosher salt

¼ teaspoon chipotle powder (or ¼ teaspoon each smoked paprika and cayenne)

To Serve

Warm corn tortillas

2 avocados, cubed

Infernal Sauce (page 36)

✦ *1 small bottle squeck juice*

1. Fill a chimney starter with charcoal, then pack the bottom with newspaper or crumpled brown paper bags. Light the starter and wait for the coals to light all the way through. The coals are ready to use once they are glowing and coated in ash. While the coals light, brush a thin layer of neutral oil on the grill grate (or spray with cooking spray meant for use with a grill). Dump the coals in an even layer on the bottom of your grill. Place the grill grate over the coals, cover the grill, and allow to preheat for about 5 minutes. If using a gas grill, oil the grates, light the burners on high, and allow the grill to preheat for about 5 minutes.

2. While the charcoal lights, toss the shrimp in a large bowl together with the paprika, onion powder, salt, cumin, garlic powder, thyme, oregano, oil, and lime juice and zest. Set aside.

3. Place the shredded red and green cabbage in a large bowl and massage vigorously with your hands to tenderise it. Whisk together the crema, lime juice, salt, and chipotle powder in a small bowl. Drizzle over the cabbage and toss to coat. Season to taste with additional salt if needed.

4. Grease a perforated grill pan or griddle with neutral oil, then place over the hottest part of the grill. Let preheat until the oil is smoking, then place the shrimp in a single layer on the pan or griddle. Let sit for 2 minutes, until lightly charred, then cook, stirring occasionally, for an additional 3 to 4 minutes, until the shrimp are opaque all the way through. Remember: Just because these are called 'blackened shrimp' doesn't mean you should burn them to a crisp—a little light charring is okay. Serve with slaw, warm corn tortillas, cubed avocado, and Infernal Sauce.

To cook on a range, prepare the shrimp and slaw as directed, then heat 2 tablespoons neutral oil in a large skillet over high heat. Cook the shrimp in two batches, sauteing each batch for about 5 to 7 minutes, until completely opaque. In addition, while you can leave the tails on for a beautiful presentation, peeled shrimp is ideal for this recipe—the tails aren't always pleasant.

LOBSTER / *Grilled Lobster*

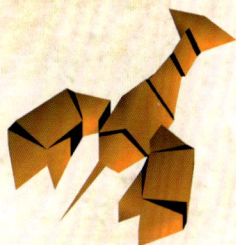

As lobster is a mainstay dish in many of the kingdom's higher-end establishments, novice cooks shouldn't shy away from preparing this notoriously difficult crustacean. This simple process of coal grilling will make your guests believe they are dining on the main street of Varrock, even if it's a boring Tuesday in Edgeville.

One word of caution, however . . .

Should you ever be tempted to make a dish which combines lobster and jubbly, please do all Gielinor a favour and find another use for your poultry. Though no one has yet determined the exact arcane conditions necessary for their summoning, jubsters can only appear in the presence of both lobster and jubbly meat. Until the mystery has been solved, it is best to keep the two ingredients separated, lest you inadvertently invite a monstrosity into your kitchen.

YIELD: *Serves 4* | PREP TIME: *35 minutes* | COOK TIME: *10 minutes* | DIFFICULTY: *Intermediate*

Equipment

Chimney starter, BBQ or grill, small saucepan

176 grams (1 cup) ghee

1 shallot, minced

2 cloves garlic, minced

1 teaspoon dill leaves, finely chopped

1 teaspoon fresh coriander/cilantro leaves, finely chopped

½ teaspoon oregano leaves, finely chopped

Juice and zest of 1 lemon

½ teaspoon coarse sea/kosher salt

4 raw lobsters, about 675 grams (1½ pounds) each

4 tablespoons neutral oil, such as rapeseed/canola or safflower

Lemon wedges

◆ *5 or 6 ripe jangerberries*

1. Fill a chimney starter with charcoal, then pack the bottom with newspaper or crumpled brown paper bags. Light the starter and wait for the coals to light all the way through. The coals are ready to use once they are glowing and coated in ash. While the coals light, brush a thin layer of neutral oil on the grill grate (or spray with cooking spray meant for use with a grill). Dump the coals in an even layer on the bottom of your grill. Place the grill grate over the coals, cover the grill, and allow to preheat for about 5 minutes. If using a gas grill, oil the grates, light the burners on high, and allow the grill to preheat for about 5 minutes.

2. While the charcoal lights, melt the ghee in a small saucepan over medium heat. Add the shallot and garlic and cook, stirring constantly, until softened and fragrant, about 3 minutes. Add the herbs, lemon juice and zest, and salt, then remove from heat.

3. On a large cutting board, cut the lobsters in half lengthwise, remove the rubber bands from the claws, then brush all over with 1 tablespoon oil. Repeat with the remaining lobsters. Note: Do this immediately before grilling—this is not a step you can do very far in advance.

4. Grill the lobsters, cut-side down, for 3 to 5 minutes, until lightly charred and opaque. Flip, drizzle with half the herb butter, and cook, covered, for 3 to 5 more minutes, until the tail meat is completely opaque but still tender. Serve immediately with the remaining herb butter and lemon wedges.

STUFFED SNAKE / *Börek*

Although there may be many ways to skin a snake, there's only one way to stuff them in Ape Atoll. Formulated for the most refined palates of the primate world, the original version features red bananas, tchiki nut paste, and a fresh raw snake for a centrepiece dish as delicious as it is stunning. A few key substitutions, as shown here, can easily transform this adaptable meal to suit any region in Gielinor.

YIELD: *Serves 8 to 10* | PREP TIME: *60 minutes* | COOK TIME: *55 minutes* | DIFFICULTY: *Master*

Equipment

Large frying pan/skillet, 46-by-33- centimetre (18-by-13-inch) baking tray/half-sheet pan

1 tablespoon extra-virgin olive oil

450 grams (1 pound) ground lamb

1 medium brown/yellow onion, finely chopped

4 cloves garlic, minced

2 teaspoons coarse sea/kosher salt

2 teaspoons ground cumin

2 teaspoons sweet paprika

1 teaspoon ground coriander seeds

1 teaspoon cinnamon

1 teaspoon Aleppo pepper flakes

½ teaspoon allspice

½ teaspoon fresh black pepper

¼ teaspoon ground clove

236 millilitres (1 cup) tomato purée

75 grams (½ cup) pine nuts, toasted

75 grams (½ cup) dried cherries, roughly chopped

1 large egg

118 millilitres (½ cup) plain kefir

10 sheets frozen phyllo pastry, thawed

3 tablespoons unsalted butter, melted

1 big snake

1. Heat the olive oil in a large skillet over medium-high heat until just shimmering. Add the ground lamb and cook, breaking apart and stirring occasionally, until well browned and just beginning to crisp, about 10 minutes.

2. Stir in the chopped onion and cook, stirring occasionally, until softened and somewhat translucent, about 7 minutes longer. Add the garlic, salt, cumin, paprika, coriander, cinnamon, pepper flakes, allspice, black pepper, and clove and cook, stirring constantly, until fragrant, about 2 minutes longer.

3. Add the tomato purée, pine nuts, and dried cherries. Reduce the heat to a simmer and cook until the moisture has mostly cooked off, about 10 to 15 minutes longer. The mixture should be moist and somewhat saucy but not watery. Remove from heat, season with additional salt if needed, and let cool to room temperature.

4. Heat the oven to 205°C (400°F) and line a half-sheet pan with parchment paper. Whisk together the egg and kefir in a small bowl. Lay the phyllo pastry next to your work surface and cover with a clean, cool, damp kitchen towel.

5. Lay a sheet of parchment paper on a clean work surface. Carefully lay 1 sheet of phyllo pastry on the parchment. Brush a very thin layer of the egg-and-kefir mixture over the pastry (work quickly, and don't worry about coating the entire surface). Lay another sheet of phyllo on top of pastry and brush with the egg mixture. Repeat the process until you've layered and brushed 5 sheets of phyllo.

6. Spoon half of the filling in an even log lengthwise across the lower quarter of the phyllo. Very carefully roll the pastry over the filling into a log. Lift the pastry using the parchment and carefully slide the filled phyllo log, seam-side down, onto the prepared baking sheet. Gently shape the log into a loose coil.

7. Repeat step 5 with the remaining phyllo pastry, egg-and-kefir mixture, and filling. This time, when you transfer the filled pastry to the prepared sheet pan, line one end of the filled pastry with the end of the coil, gently push the ends into each other, then coil the second filled pastry around the first to form one large coil.

8. Brush the börek all over with melted butter, then bake for 45 to 55 minutes, or until the pastry is deeply golden, crisp, and flaky. Let cool slightly, then cut and serve.

COOKED JUBBLY / *Fire-Roasted Chicken*

◆◆◆

This ogre delicacy hails from the Feldip Hills south of Yanille, where a set of wrong directions landed me deep within hostile territory. Quite fortunate for me that my first encounter was with a fellow chef by the name of Rantz Sr., who not only ensured my safety but was willing to share the secrets to hunting and cooking what he called 'big flappers'. He also carried with him the most charming feathered hats . . .

Don't discount the rustic preparation of this dish; the results will be a surprisingly succulent dish, whether you use regular chompy or the rarer jubbly birds.

YIELD: *Serves 4* | PREP TIME: *35 minutes, plus 4 to 12 hours for marinating* | COOK TIME: *65 minutes* | DIFFICULTY: *Intermediate*

Equipment

Blender, chimney starter, BBQ or grill, meat thermometer

1 whole chicken, about 1.8 to 2.25 kilograms (4 to 5 pounds)

1 tablespoon coarse sea/kosher salt

1 tablespoon fresh thyme leaves

2 teaspoons smoked paprika

1 teaspoon fresh black pepper

1 large white onion, peeled and quartered

6 cloves garlic, peeled

Juice and zest of 3 lemons

60 millilitres (¼ cup) neutral oil, such as rapeseed/canola or safflower

✦ *4 or 5 wimpy feathers*

This recipe's method cooks chicken faster and more evenly and creates a crispier skin, but for the photo presentation, add 10 to 20 minutes to the cook time. Use your instant-read thermometer to test when it's done.

To prepare in the oven or range, roast at 450°F on an oven-proof wire rack set in a sheet tray for 55 to 65 minutes.

1. Place the chicken on a cutting board, breast-side down. Using sharp kitchen shears, cut along one side. Repeat on the other side of the backbone. Flip the chicken over, splay out the thighs and legs, and press down on the upper part of the breasts to break the wishbone and force the chicken to lay flat. Place the chicken in a large zip-top bag. Discard the backbone, or freeze it in an airtight container to save for making stock.

2. Place the remaining ingredients into a blender and purée until smooth. If needed, add more oil to thin the marinade out. Pour into the bag with the chicken, then seal the bag most of the way. Squeeze out as much air as possible, then seal the bag the rest of the way. Squeeze the bag to distribute the marinade, then place in a bowl in case the bag leaks. Chill for at least 4 hours, or up to 12.

3. Fill a chimney starter with charcoal, then pack the bottom with newspaper or crumpled brown paper bags. Light the starter and wait for the coals to light all the way through. The coals are ready to use once they are glowing and coated in ash. While the coals light, brush a thin layer of neutral oil on the grill grate (or spray with cooking spray meant for use with a grill). Dump the coals in an even layer on one side of your grill to create a hot zone and a cool zone. Place the grill grate over the coals, cover the grill, and allow to preheat for about 5 minutes. If using a gas grill, oil the grates, light half of the burners on high, and allow the grill to preheat for about 5 minutes. Immediately before transferring the chicken to the grill, throw two large chunks of smoking wood (cherry, hickory, apple, etc.) onto the lit coals.

4. Remove the chicken from the bag and gently pat dry with paper towels to remove excess marinade. Place the chicken on the cool side of the grill, breast-side up, with the legs pointing towards the hot side. Cover the grill and open all the air vents. Let cook, covered, for 45 to 60 minutes, until an instant-read thermometer registers 74°C (165°F) when inserted into the thickest part of the breast. By now, the skin should be quite golden and crisp. If you desire more caramelisation, flip the chicken over onto the hot side of the grill and let char for 3 to 5 minutes before serving.

COOKED MEAT / Carne Asada

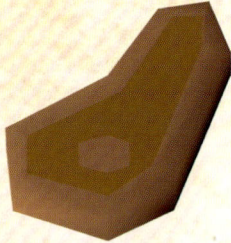

Some claim cooking meat is an art, whereas others insist it's a matter of science. What if I told you it could be a tool of the arcane as well?

It is well known that food can elicit strong emotions which can in turn enhance the casting of certain spells, but I once met a witch in Rimmington who could also increase one's magic by way of a specific meaty broth. To entertain my curiosity, I brought her the requested rat's tail, burnt meat, eye of newt, and an onion to see if her claims were true.

I'm sure you can imagine my absolute surprise when the very next dish I made from a tough piece of steak, an orange, and some spices turned into this delicious recipe. Magical indeed!

YIELD: *Serves 8* | PREP TIME: *50 minutes, plus 4 to 8 hours marinating* | COOK TIME: *10 minutes* | DIFFICULTY: *Intermediate*

Equipment

Blender, chimney starter, BBQ or grill, meat thermometer

Carne Asada

60 millilitres (¼ cup) Spicy Sauce (page 35) OR 47 grams (½ cup) ancho chilli powder plus 1 chipotle pepper in adobo sauce

60 millilitres (¼ cup) neutral oil, such as rapeseed/canola or safflower

85 grams (½ cup) fresh pineapple chunks

Juice and zest of 3 oranges

Juice and zest of 4 limes

2 tablespoons agave syrup

1 small brown/yellow onion, peeled and quartered

½ bunch fresh coriander/cilantro leaves and tender stems

1 jalapeño, stem removed

8 cloves garlic, peeled

1 tablespoon coarse sea/kosher salt

Ingredients continued on next page

1. Place the Spicy Sauce, oil, pineapple, orange juice and zest, lime juice and zest, agave syrup, onion, coriander/cilantro, jalapeño, garlic, salt, cumin, ground coriander, black pepper, and oregano into a blender. Purée until smooth, about 2 to 4 minutes.

2. Place the steak in a plastic bag with a zip top and pour the marinade all over. Seal the bag most of the way, squeeze out as much air as possible, then seal the rest of the way. Place the bag in a bowl in case of leaks, and chill for 4 to 8 hours.

3. Fill a chimney starter with charcoal, then pack the bottom with newspaper or crumpled brown paper bags. Light the starter and wait for the coals to light all the way through. The coals are ready to use once they are glowing and coated in ash. While the coals light, brush a thin layer of neutral oil on the grill grate (or spray with cooking spray meant for use with a grill). Dump the coals in an even layer on the bottom of your grill. Place the grill grate over the coals, cover the grill, and allow to preheat for about 5 minutes. If using a gas grill, oil the grates, light the burners on high, and allow the grill to preheat for about 5 minutes.

*Recipe continued on next page

1 tablespoon ground cumin

2 teaspoons ground coriander seeds

1 teaspoon ground black pepper

1 teaspoon Mexican oregano

1.36 kilograms (3 pounds) flank or skirt steak

To Serve

Warm corn tortillas

Spicy Sauce (page 35)

Infernal Sauce (page 36)

Cotija cheese

Lime wedges

Chopped fresh coriander/cilantro

✦ *1 bushel bruma herb*

4. Wipe excess marinade from the steak and grill for 3 to 5 minutes on each side, until lightly charred and an instant-read thermometer registers 46°C (115°F) when inserted into the thickest part of the steak. Transfer to a cutting board and let rest for 5 to 10 minutes, then slice against the grain. Serve with corn tortillas, Spicy Sauce and/or Infernal Sauce, cotija cheese, lime wedges, and coriander/cilantro.

To prepare this dish on a range, follow the marinating instructions, wipe excess marinade from the steak, and gently pat dry with paper towels. Cook in three batches in a cast-iron skillet with 2 tablespoons neutral oil on high heat for 3 to 5 minutes on each side, until an instant-read thermometer registers 43° to 46°C (110 to 115°F) when inserted into the thickest part of the steak. The steak will continue to cook while resting, increasing the temperature. Aim for 46°C (115°F) before resting for rare, 52°C (125°F) for medium-rare, 57°C (135°F) for medium, 63°C (145°F) for medium-well, and 68°C (155°F) for well done.

WILD PIE / *Game Pie*

Preparations of this provincial dish come to us from archers seeking a hearty meal from the successes of their hunts. As available game changes from location to location, so too can the contents of Wild Pie. They most commonly include either chompy or oomlie, along with rabbit and bear.

Although the version I offer exchanges some of the original's rustic charm for ease of a range, it more than makes up for it with the rich flavour of properly seared meat.

YIELD: *Serves 8* | PREP TIME: *20 minutes* | COOK TIME: *2 hours* | DIFFICULTY: *Intermediate*

Equipment

20-centimetre (8-inch) springform pan/cake tin, small frying pan/skillet, small saucepan

Filling

1.8 kilograms (4 pounds) mixed boneless game meat (such as partridge, quail, wild boar, rabbit, and pheasant), diced

8 ounces pancetta, diced

2 shallots, minced

6 cloves garlic, minced

1 tablespoon coarse sea/kosher salt

1 teaspoon fresh black pepper

½ teaspoon ground mace

3 tablespoons fresh thyme leaves, chopped

1 tablespoon fresh rosemary leaves, chopped

2 teaspoons fresh sage leaves, chopped

75 grams (½ cup) dried cherries, roughly chopped

Crust

600 grams (5 cups) plain/all-purpose flour

4 tablespoons unsalted butter

8 tablespoons lard, plus more for greasing the pan

236 millilitres (1 cup) water

1½ teaspoons coarse sea/kosher salt

1 large egg

1 tablespoon milk

✦ *2 teaspoons crushed dragonstone*

1. Preheat the oven to 205°C (400°F) and place the oven rack in the centre position. Grease a 20-centimetre (8-inch) springform cake pan with lard and set aside.

2. Toss together the game meat, pancetta, shallots, garlic, salt, pepper, mace, thyme, rosemary, sage, and dried cherries in a large bowl until the ingredients are well combined and evenly distributed. Take a small scoop of the filling and fry in a small skillet with 1 teaspoon oil over medium-high heat until cooked through. Taste, and adjust the seasoning of the filling as desired.

3. Pour the flour into a large bowl. Add the butter, lard, water, and salt to a small saucepan and bring to a full rolling boil over high heat. Immediately pour the mixture into the flour and stir with a wooden spoon until a smooth dough forms. Allow the dough to cool until safe to handle, but don't let it cool too much—this type of dough becomes very brittle as it cools.

4. Roll ¾ of the dough out into a large circle a bit thicker than 6 millimetres (¼ inch), then press into the prepared cake pan. If it tears, patch holes or tears with a piece of dough. Trim overhang down to about 1.25 centimetres (½ inch). Pour the filling into the crust, lightly packing it down by hand.

5. Roll out the remaining dough to a roughly 23-centimetre (9-inch) circle. Lay the top crust on top of the filling, press the edges of the top and bottom crusts together, then crimp them. Cut out a 2.5-centimetre (1-inch) circle from the centre of the top crust to allow steam to escape.

6. Beat together the egg and milk in a small bowl, then brush the mixture onto the top of the piecrust. Place the cake pan onto a baking sheet to catch any overflowing juices, then bake for 30 minutes. Reduce the heat to 177°C (350°F) and bake for an additional 90 minutes, or until the top crust is deeply golden and the internal temperature of the pie reaches 74°C (165°F). Allow to cool to room temperature in the pan, then serve.

ROAST BEAST MEAT / *Beef Satay*

◆◆◆

Roast Beast Meat is a common request at Lumbridge Castle due to the duke's love of hunting. Although considered more a preparation method than a strict recipe, the commonality is small, free-range game, such as kebbits, served roasted on either a spit or individual skewers.

If you find yourself craving Roast Beast Meat outside of hunting season, I have been known to ask local farmers for their most ferocious chickens and have seldom been disappointed by the results. When you serve these skewers alongside a delectable peanut sauce, all you'll find at the end of the meal are empty plates and content belly pats.

YIELD: *Serves 4 to 6* | PREP TIME: *1 hour, plus 1 to 8 hours to marinate* | COOK TIME: *3 minutes* | DIFFICULTY: *Novice*

Equipment

Blender, mortar and pestle or food processor, small saucepan, chimney starter, BBQ or grill

Beef Satay Skewers

450 to 675 grams (1 to 1½ pounds) sirloin steak, fat trimmed

118 millilitres (½ cup) coconut milk

60 millilitres (¼ cup) neutral oil, such as rapeseed/canola or safflower

60 millilitres (¼ cup) fresh coriander/cilantro leaves

2 tablespoons white vinegar

2 teaspoons ground coriander

2 teaspoons ground turmeric

2 teaspoons ground cumin

1 stalk lemongrass, sliced

3 spring onions/scallions, white and light green parts only, roughly chopped

2 tablespoons soy sauce

2 tablespoons fish sauce

1 tablespoon fresh grated galangal (or ginger)

1 tablespoon palm sugar (or brown sugar)

1. Place the steak in the freezer for about 15 minutes until somewhat firm. Slice the steak into 6-millimetre-thin (¼-inch-thin) strips roughly 10 centimetres long by 4 centimetres wide (4-by-1½ inches). Place in a plastic bag.

2. Place the coconut milk, oil, coriander/cilantro, vinegar, ground coriander, turmeric, cumin, lemongrass, spring onions/scallions, soy sauce, fish sauce, galangal, and palm sugar in a blender. Purée until smooth, about 3 to 5 minutes, then pour over the steak. Seal the bag most of the way, squeeze out as much air as possible, then seal the rest of the way. Place in a bowl in case the bag leaks, then let sit for 1 hour, or up to 8. If marinating for more than 1 hour, store in the fridge until ready to cook.

3. Meanwhile, make the peanut sauce. Grind the peanuts into a fine meal (with some larger chunks of peanuts still visible) with a mortar and pestle or food processor. If using the latter, be careful not to grind into peanut butter.

4. Scoop the fat from the top of the coconut milk and into a small saucepan. Heat over medium-high until melted, then add the red curry paste. Let cook until fragrant and bubbling, about 2 to 4 minutes, then add the rest of the coconut milk. Reduce heat to medium, then add the ground peanuts, tamarind paste, palm sugar, fish sauce, and soy sauce. Adjust the flavouring to your liking with more palm sugar, fish sauce, or soy sauce, then remove from heat and squeeze the lime juice over.

Bamboo skewers, soaked in water for 1 hour

Peanut Sauce

100 grams (¾ cup) roasted peanuts

236 millilitres (1 cup) coconut milk

2 tablespoons red curry paste

3 tablespoons tamarind paste

3 tablespoons palm sugar (or brown sugar)

1 tablespoon fish sauce

1 tablespoon soy sauce

Juice of 1 lime

✦ *1 sprig avantoe*

5. Fill a chimney starter with charcoal, then pack the bottom with newspaper or crumpled brown paper bags. Light the starter and wait for the coals to light all the way through. The coals are ready to use once they are glowing and coated in ash. While the coals light, brush a thin layer of neutral oil on the grill grate (or spray with cooking spray meant for use with a grill). Dump the coals in an even layer on the bottom of your grill. Place the grill grate over the coals, cover the grill, and allow to preheat for about 5 minutes. If using a gas grill, oil the grates, light the burners on high, and allow the grill to preheat for about 5 minutes.

6. While the charcoal heats, thread 2 or 3 strips of steak onto each skewer, allowing the steak to bunch up slightly.

7. Grill the skewers for 2 minutes, until lightly charred, then flip and grill for 1 additional minute, until cooked through. Serve with peanut sauce.

TERRIBLE PIE / *Crawfish Pie*

◆ ◆

One of the things which helps keep my passion going in the kitchen is a yearly tradition of seeking culinary challenges from chefs elsewhere in Gielinor. Five years ago, I was tasked by the chef of the Pick and Lute pub in Taverley to make an inspired version of the infamously Terrible Pie they serve on occasion to unscrupulous individuals.

This mouthwatering version stays true to the pie's origins with the use of crayfish, potato, and a pie shell—though whether you use the manky, stinking, and maggoty varieties is up to you.

YIELD: *Serves 6 to 8* | PREP TIME: *45 minutes* | COOK TIME: *1 hour* | DIFFICULTY: *Intermediate*

Equipment

Food processor, large Dutch oven, 23-centimetre (9-inch) pie dish/plate

Piecrust

300 grams (2½ cups) plain/all-purpose flour

16 tablespoons cold unsalted butter, cut into 1.25-centimetre (½-inch) cubes

1 teaspoon coarse sea/kosher salt

78 millilitres (⅓ cup) ice-cold water

Filling

4 tablespoons unsalted butter

2 tablespoons neutral oil, such as rapeseed/canola or safflower

30 grams (¼ cup) plain/all-purpose flour

1 brown/yellow onion, finely chopped

1 green bell pepper, diced

3 stalks celery, minced

6 cloves garlic, minced

1 tablespoon Old Bay seasoning

177 millilitres (¾ cup) seafood stock

Ingredients continued on next page

1. Place the flour, butter, and kosher salt in the bowl of a food processor. Pulse until the texture of wet sand, about 2 minutes. Tip the mixture into a large bowl and add the ice water. Mix with a wooden spoon or stiff rubber spatula until moistened through and no dry flour remains. Add 1 to 2 tablespoons of cold water if the dough is too dry. Divide the dough in half, shape into two discs, and tightly wrap with cling film/plastic wrap. Chill for at least 1 hour.

2. Heat the butter and oil together in a large Dutch oven over medium heat until the butter is melted. Add the flour and cook, stirring constantly, until the roux is lightly toasted to a tan colour and smells nutty, about 10 to 15 minutes.

3. Add the onion, bell pepper, and celery and cook, stirring frequently, until softened, about 7 to 10 minutes. Add the garlic and Old Bay seasoning and cook, stirring constantly, until fragrant, about 1 minute longer. Stir in the seafood stock and cream and let simmer, stirring occasionally, until thickened to a gravy consistency, about 15 to 20 minutes. Stir in the cooked crayfish tails and remove from heat. Let cool to room temperature.

4. Heat the oven to 205°C (400°F) and place the oven rack in the lower-third position. Roll one of the discs of pie dough out to a circle about 6 millimetres (¼ inch) thick on a liberally floured work surface. Carefully transfer to a deep 23-centimetre (9-inch) pie plate, allowing the dough to fill the plate with at least 2.5 centimetres (1 inch) of overhang. Transfer to the fridge while you roll out the top crust. Repeat the rolling process with the remaining dough.

Recipe continued on next page

118 millilitres (½ cup) double/heavy cream

1 Baked Potato (page 41), cut into bite-size pieces

450 grams (1 pound) frozen, peeled, and cooked crayfish/crawfish tails, thawed

1 large egg

1 tablespoon milk

◆ *1 fistful expensive spices*

5. Transfer the filling to the dough-lined pie plate. Beat the egg and milk together in a small bowl. Brush the edges of the dough, then carefully transfer the top crust to the pie plate. Trim the overhang to about 1.25 centimetres (½ inch), then fold the overhang over itself and crimp to seal.

6. Slice two slits in the centre of the top crust to allow steam to escape. Brush the entire surface of the crust with egg wash. Place the pie plate on a baking sheet and bake for 45 minutes to 1 hour, until the crust is deep golden brown and the filling is bubbling. Allow to cool for about 15 to 20 minutes before serving.

This pie is typically made with foul, manky seafood and the most spoiled ingredients you can find—ideal, of course, for poisoning someone. When you make this dish for friends, ensure your ingredients are fresh.

TUNA AND CORN / *Seared Tuna Steak with Esquites*

A passion for cooking usually starts with a memorable meal and a desire to repeat that experience in your own kitchen. We seek to learn recipes and master techniques, yet something is often missing in our early attempts to re-create the magic of a particular dish. When our Lumbridge apprentices hit this plateau, I take them out to the farm to understand the importance of quality ingredients.

Sweetcorn and tuna take centre stage in this dish, so special attention must be given to obtaining the freshest and most well-tended ingredients. This means selecting ears which were lovingly protected by scarecrows, spices which are fresh and flavourful, and tuna which is fresh and responsibly caught. I encourage new chefs to always identify their primary components and ensure most of their budget is spent there first.

YIELD: *Serves 4* | PREP TIME: *35 minutes* | COOK TIME: *20 minutes* | DIFFICULTY: *Intermediate*

Equipment

23-by-23-centimetre (9-by-9-inch) glass or ceramic baking dish, chimney starter, BBQ or grill

Tuna Steaks

4 tuna steaks, about 6 ounces each

2 tablespoons neutral oil, such as rapeseed/canola or safflower

1½ teaspoons sea/kosher salt

1 teaspoon fresh black pepper

1 teaspoon ancho chilli powder

Juice of 2 limes

Esquites

60 millilitres (¼ cup) mayonnaise

60 millilitres (¼ cup) Mexican crema

30 grams (¼ cup) cotija cheese, crumbled

2 tablespoons fresh coriander/cilantro leaves, minced

2 tablespoons ancho chilli powder

1 teaspoon coarse sea/kosher salt

*Ingredients continued on next page

1. Fill a chimney starter with charcoal, then pack the bottom with newspaper or crumpled brown paper bags. Light the starter and wait for the coals to light all the way through. The coals are ready to use once they are glowing and coated in ash. While the coals light, brush a thin layer of neutral oil on the grill grate (or spray with cooking spray meant for use with a grill). Dump the coals in an even layer on the bottom of your grill. Place the grill grate over the coals, cover the grill, and allow to preheat for about 5 minutes. If using a gas grill, oil the grates, light the burners on high, and allow the grill to preheat for about 5 minutes.

2. While the charcoal lights, place the tuna steaks in a single layer in a 23-by-23-centimetre (9-by-9-inch) baking dish. Drizzle with oil, then season the steaks all over both sides with the salt, pepper, ancho chilli powder, and lime juice. Let sit until the grill is ready, turning once or twice so both sides of the tuna soak up the seasoning.

3. Stir the mayonnaise, crema, cotija, fresh coriander/cilantro, ancho chilli powder, salt, pepper, chipotle powder, and lime juice and zest together in a large bowl until well mixed. Season to taste with additional salt and lime juice, if needed.

4. Brush the corn with oil all over, then grill, turning occasionally, until the corn is well charred and tender, about 10 minutes altogether. Remove from heat and allow to cool until safe enough to handle.

*Recipe continued on next page

½ teaspoon fresh black pepper

½ teaspoon chipotle powder (or ¼ teaspoon each smoked paprika and cayenne)

Juice and zest of 2 limes

4 ears fresh corn, shucked (i.e., with the leaves and fibres removed)

2 tablespoons neutral oil, such as rapeseed/canola or safflower

To Serve

Lime wedges

Fresh coriander/cilantro leaves, chopped

✦ *2 leaves grimy arbuck*

You can acquire fresh fish from your local fishmonger, from markets, or from a few locations throughout Gielinor, such as Harry's Fishing Shop, Lovecraft's Tackle, and Gerrant's Fishy Business!

When selecting a fish, look for clear eyes (not dull or sunken), a metallic shine and robust colour, and a fresh, mild scent. Whether you're buying a whole fish or a fillet, it should have firm flesh which springs back quickly when pressed.

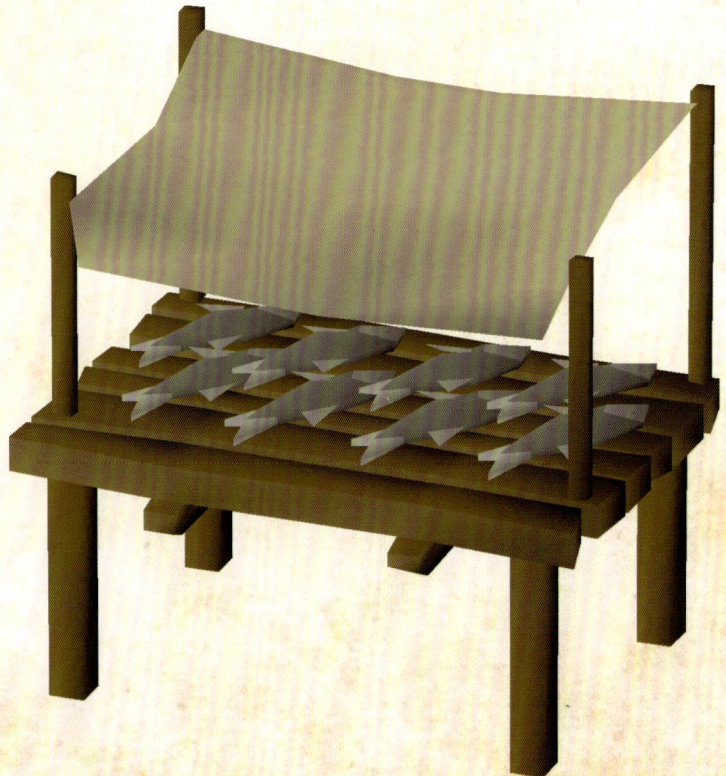

5. Hold an ear of corn upright on a large cutting board and use a sharp chef's knife to cut the kernels off. Repeat with the remaining ears of corn, then transfer the kernels to the bowl of mayo mixture. Toss to combine, then set aside in a warm place.

6. Pat the tuna steaks dry with paper towels, then grill for about 2 to 3 minutes on each side until slightly charred but still rare in the middle. If you prefer well-cooked tuna steaks, cook for 5 or 6 minutes on each side.

7. Divide the esquites evenly amongst 4 shallow bowls, place a tuna steak on top of the esquites, and garnish with lime wedges and fresh coriander/cilantro. Serve immediately.

CURRY / *Japanese Curry*

Much like stew, curry typically begins as a blank palette of water, potatoes, and meat, after which the spices create the flavourful soul of the dish. This preparation is my favourite go-to for banquets—it's beautifully spiced, delicately sweet, not too hot, not too sweet, and creates a beautiful broth upon which a dried curry leaf can be floated to great effect.

    This is also the prime recipe for training new cooks in the Lumbridge kitchen when we have an abundance of ingredients, as it provides a wealth of experience without requiring much in the way of foreknowledge.

YIELD: *Serves 6 to 8* | **PREP TIME:** *15 minutes* | **COOK TIME:** *1 hour* | **DIFFICULTY:** *Intermediate*

Equipment
Small saucepan, large Dutch oven

Roux

8 tablespoons unsalted butter

60 grams (½ cup) plain/all-purpose flour

4 tablespoons Japanese curry powder

1 teaspoon ground cumin

½ teaspoon ground coriander

½ teaspoon fresh black pepper

½ teaspoon ground mustard

¼ teaspoon cinnamon

¼ teaspoon cardamom

¼ teaspoon ground clove

Curry

2 tablespoons ghee or neutral oil, such as rapeseed/canola or safflower

3 brown/yellow onions, roughly chopped

1 Fuji apple, peeled, cored, and grated

1 tablespoon fresh grated ginger

4 cloves garlic, minced

900 grams (2 pounds) boneless, skinless chicken thighs

1. Melt the butter in a small saucepan over medium-low heat. Once fully melted and foaming, add the flour and cook, stirring constantly, until it turns the colour of peanut butter, about 10 to 15 minutes. Add the spices and cook, stirring constantly, until fragrant, about 1 minute longer. Remove from heat and set aside.

2. Heat the ghee in a large Dutch oven over medium-high heat until melted. Add the onions and cook, stirring occasionally, until translucent and beginning to brown on the edges, about 10 to 15 minutes. Add the apple, ginger, and garlic and cook, stirring constantly, until fragrant, about 1 to 2 minutes longer.

3. Add the remaining ingredients and bring to a boil. The chicken and vegetables should be just barely submerged in the chicken stock, but if there's not quite enough to submerge them, add a bit more stock or water if needed. Reduce to a simmer, cover, and cook for about 20 minutes, or until the potatoes are just barely tender—they should offer some resistance when poked with a sharp knife or fork. As the pot simmers, check it after the 10-minute mark and skim off any foam or scum accumulated at the top of the liquid and discard. Repeat every 5 minutes.

4. Ladle out about 236 millilitres (1 cup) of stock from the Dutch oven and into the prepared curry roux. Whisk until smooth, and then add the mix to the Dutch oven. Cook, stirring occasionally, until thickened and the potatoes and carrots are completely tender, about 10 to 15 minutes longer. Remove and discard the curry leaves and bay leaves. Season to taste with additional salt, if needed. Serve immediately with cooked Japanese rice.

4 carrots, peeled and cut into bite-size chunks

4 Yukon gold potatoes (or other waxy varieties, such as Charlotte), peeled and cut into bite-size chunks

0.95 litre (1 quart) chicken stock

2 sprigs fresh or frozen curry leaves

2 bay leaves

2 tablespoons honey or maple syrup

2 tablespoons soy sauce

2 tablespoons mirin

1 tablespoon coarse sea/kosher salt

Cooked Japanese rice, to serve

◆ *1 tablespoon 'spice'*

Bay leaves are often suggested as substitutes for curry leaves, but the flavour is quite different. Dried or frozen curry leaves work in a pinch, but nothing compares to the aroma of fresh leaves.

Fresh curry leaves can be sourced from Indian supermarkets and from most modern general stores; you can likely have them delivered to your front door!

PUDDINGS

THE GOBLIN GENERALS

Who doesn't like a two-for-one? What, you don't? Why does this not surprise me? Regardless, if we intend to beat the Culinaromancer, then you will have to find the perfect dish General Bentnoze and General Wartface can agree upon. No, we are not DOOMED—not until we get around to freeing Evil Dave, in any case.

Thanks to your mediation some years back, we know they're quite particular about colours. Though we have the generals to thank for Gielinor's recent renaissance in battlefield fashion, what we need is an expert in goblin cooking. Head north of Falador to Goblin Village and seek out Mudknuckles to see if he still has the recipe for his infamous Slop of Compromise. With any luck, you'll catch him before he sets off on tour to promote his new best-selling cookbook, Fast Food: Eat Well or Die Trying.

SIR AMIK VARZE

So, what if I told you that the key to saving Sir Amik Varze is an evil chicken? Yes, chickens can be quite evil, what with their beady little eyes and malevolent shrines. Look, you don't have to take my word for it; there are entire books written on the subject—go read one. Or better yet, why don't you go and get the evil egg we need without wasting so much time? And get some Kharazi vanilla, dramen cinnamon, and sweetcorn while you're at it.

Once you source and mix the ingredients for the Brûlée Supreme, you must get it flambéed by begging, tricking, or killing a dragon which just so happens to be holding the token of a fairy dragon which is bound to grant you one request. Yes, that might seem oddly specific, but trust me, it works.

Now, I don't have to tell you that Sir Amik Varze is an important man, and that without his righteous example of virtue and glory, all Gielinor could fall to darkness. What? Of course he's that important! He and his White Knights fought alongside Saradomin against Zamorak himself. Don't adventurers learn their history anymore? Wait, you're not still mad that he's friends with Evil Dave, are you? Come on, that young man's really not such a bad egg.

Sorry, I couldn't resist. But hey, listen, if you happen to visit the wise old man in Draynor to learn more about this evil chicken business, do me a favour and tell him Bubbykins says hello. No, you may not ask why.

SLOP OF COMPROMISE
Orange Almond Bread Pudding

When cooking for foreign dignitaries, the goal is to expose guests to the bounty of Misthalin while also offering them familiar comforts from their homelands. A chef may even attempt a fusion dish which blends the flavours of multiple lands into something evoking a spirit of cooperation and peace.

When this dish was presented to a goblin delegation as a celebratory bread pudding, one goblin fondly likened it to a beloved recipe known as Slop of Compromise. I took no offence to the name—nor to their excitement that the almond flakes bore resemblance to the 'maggots' his mother used in her own recipe.

YIELD: *Serves 10 to 12* | PREP TIME: *1 hour* | COOK TIME: *50 minutes* | DIFFICULTY: *Novice*

Equipment

Oven-safe wire cooling rack, 46-by-33-centimetre (18-by-13-inch) baking tray/half-sheet pan, 23-by-33-centimetre (9-by-13-inch) glass or ceramic baking dish

1 loaf brioche (about 450 grams or 1 pound), sliced

150 grams (1 cup) dried cherries

100 grams (1 cup) flaked/slivered almonds, toasted, divided

175 grams (1 cup) dark chocolate chips

473 millilitres (2 cups) double/heavy cream

236 millilitres (1 cup) whole milk

4 large eggs

8 tablespoons unsalted butter, melted, plus more for the baking dish

200 grams (1 cup) lightly packed light brown sugar

2 teaspoons cinnamon

Zest of 1 orange

1 tablespoon vanilla extract

½ teaspoon almond extract

½ teaspoon orange blossom water

Vanilla ice cream, to serve

✦ *1 teaspoon shredded bloodweed, for garnish*

1. Preheat the oven to 93.3°C (200°F) with a rack placed in the middle. Set an oven-safe wire cooling rack in a half-sheet pan. Line the wire rack with the slices of brioche and bake until dry and very lightly toasted, about 45 minutes. Remove and let cool, then cut into 1.25-centimetre (½-inch) cubes.

2. Increase the oven temperature to 177°C (350°F) and butter a 23-by-33-centimetre (9-by-13-inch) baking dish.

3. Toss the bread together in a large bowl with the dried cherries, ¾ of the toasted flaked/slivered almonds, and the chocolate chips.

4. Beat together the cream, whole milk, eggs, butter, brown sugar, cinnamon, orange zest, vanilla, almond extract, and orange blossom water in a medium bowl until smooth. Pour over the bread mixture and toss to combine. Pour the bread pudding into the prepared baking dish and sprinkle the remaining flaked/slivered almonds over the top.

5. Place the baking dish on a half-sheet pan and cover with aluminium foil. Bake for 45 to 50 minutes until puffed, then remove the foil and bake for 15 more minutes until golden and set. Serve hot with vanilla ice cream. It can also be enjoyed cold!

BRÛLÉE SUPREME / *No-Bake Crème Brûlée*

◆

Although the origins of Brûlée Supreme remain shrouded in mystery, accounts of what it tastes like are well documented. Creamy, with a generous dusting of ground dramen, a hint of malevolence, and a dragon-fire flambé which imparts a subtly smoky flavour. Delicious!

As most chefs lack ready access to dragons or evil chickens, this version of the infamous dish offers common substitutions without losing the dark heart of what made this the official dessert of the White Knights of Falador.

YIELD: *Serves 4* | PREP TIME: *1 hour* | COOK TIME: *10 minutes, plus 4 hours to chill* | DIFFICULTY: *Intermediate*

Equipment

Medium saucier, four 4-ounce heat-proof ramekins, kitchen torch

354 millilitres (1½ cups) double/heavy cream

118 millilitres (½ cup) whole milk

1 vanilla pod, split

1 tablespoon corn flour/cornstarch

50 grams (¼ cup) granulated sugar

¼ teaspoon coarse sea/kosher salt

5 large egg yolks

Demerara/raw sugar

◆ *5 tablespoons dragon scale dust*

Sauciers have curved bottoms, making them preferable for certain tasks where it's likely for a mixture to get trapped in the edges of a straight-sided saucepan. A saucepan is okay to use if you don't have a saucier, but you'll have to be extra vigilant and thorough with stirring so the mixture doesn't get trapped in the edges and burnt.

1. Add the cream, milk, and vanilla pod to a medium saucier. Heat over medium heat until the mixture just simmers. Remove from heat, cover, and let sit at room temperature for 30 minutes. For stronger vanilla flavour, chill the pan in the fridge for up to 24 hours.

2. Whisk together the cornstarch, sugar, and salt in a medium bowl. Whisk in the egg yolks until smooth.

3. Bring the cream mixture up to a bare simmer over medium heat. Remove from heat and discard the vanilla bean. Transfer 236 millilitres (1 cup) of the cream mixture to a measuring jug/spouted measuring cup.

4. Whisking constantly, pour a very small amount of the cream mixture into the egg yolk mixture. Repeat, adding a little of the hot cream mixture at a time, all the while whisking the egg mixture constantly, until you've added the entire cup of cream and milk.

5. Return the contents of the bowl to the saucier, whisking it in. Cook over medium-low heat, whisking constantly, until the mixture thickens and begins to bubble. Once you see the first bubble form, set a 1-minute timer. When the timer goes off, remove from heat.

6. Set a fine mesh strainer over a clean bowl. Pour the custard through the strainer. Divide the custard amongst four 4-ounce heatproof ramekins. Let cool at room temperature, then transfer to the fridge. Chill, uncovered, for at least 4 hours.

7. When you're ready to serve, sprinkle each portion with about 1 teaspoon raw sugar in an even layer. Light a kitchen torch and, holding it so the end of the flame is about 2 inches from the surface of the crème brûlée, gently melt the sugar until it forms a golden-brown crust on top of the custard. Pay close attention as you work, and take care not to scorch and burn the sugar. Let cool for 2 minutes, then serve.

CAKES AND SWEET SNACKS

MOUNTAIN DWARF

The problem with secret councils is that they're naturally so full of secrets! Take our Mountain Dwarf friend here, for example. Though I'm sure he has a good and proper name, no one has set out a name card at this banquet—thus, he is the Mountain Dwarf.

What we do know is that he hails from the mines beneath the White Wolf Mountain region which connects the towns of Catherby and Taverley. Assuming you've proven yourself worthy of passage with your ample fishing prowess, seek out the Mountain Dwarf's father, Rohak, who is the only known chef to produce the infamous dessert known as Dwarven Rock Cakes.

Be warned, however, that the old dwarf is known to be a bit of a goat. I suggest the ages-old tactic of getting him smashed—since Falador is along the way, visit the Rising Sun inn and speak to a barmaid named Emily. There, turn up the charm and persuade her to share her secret for turning Asgarnian Ale into the dwarven favourite known as Asgoldian Ale.

Oh, and remember, a dwarf's thirst is only rivaled by the hotness of his cake, so be sure to bring gloves which can handle the heat.

LUMBRIDGE SAGE

Is there any chance you were planning on hanging up your sword and board for a quiet life as a town guide anytime soon? No? Well, then, we're going to need to save Phileas next, or Lumbridge may risk losing its 'best place to start your adventuring' title.

To make the Cake of Guidance and save the Lumbridge Sage, you'll need to make a short jaunt to the mage tower located south of Draynor Village. Once there, speak with Wizard Traiborn, who happens to be the foremost expert on imbuing cakes with all sorts of esoteric knowledge. Be forewarned, however: If he asks for some eggy peggy, some floury woury, or some milky wilky, your job is to ask how many and then go find it. Laughing at, correcting, or otherwise questioning him or his choice of hat is the surest way to be turned into an amphibian. What, you thought the frogs south of Lumbridge were naturally attracted to the town? Oh, you sweet child.

In recalling your phonetic challenges during earlier adventures, I'll even give you the words for enchanting eggs, milk, and flour for a Cake of Guidance early so you can practise on your way there:

Dandolino Zadribrim!

Skalindom Ralinaplo!

Splendidium romelno!

Take care to say it correctly, or there's no telling what confectionary misfeasance may result.

CAKE, FOUR WAYS

◆◆

Celebrations demand cake, and what better recipe than one which can be easily adapted to any occasion? Here, I share the technique for making my standard yellow cake, then teach you how to elevate it with natural chocolate. After, you'll be ready to attempt the famous anniversary cake I created to honour the first Council of Lumbridge.

Lastly, I'll share my secrets for making the very wizardly Cake of Guidance, one of the only foods scientifically and arcanically proven to give you the insight necessary to know what, when, where, why, and how anyone would ever want to summon a thingummywut.

YIELD: *Serves 8 to 12* | PREP TIME: *20 minutes* | COOK TIME: *35 minutes* | DIFFICULTY: *Intermediate*

Equipment

Two 23-centimetre (9-inch) cake tins/pans, stand mixer, cake tester or toothpick

Cake

16 tablespoons unsalted butter, room temperature

400 grams (2 cups) granulated sugar

4 large eggs, room temperature

1 tablespoon vanilla extract

¾ teaspoon coarse sea/kosher salt

1 tablespoon baking powder

360 grams (3 cups) cake flour

236 millilitres (1 cup) buttermilk, room temperature

Ingredients continued on next page

If you don't have access to cake flour, whisk together 315 grams (2 5/8 cups) all-purpose flour and 42 grams (6 tablespoons) cornflour/cornstarch to get about 360 grams (3 cups) cake flour.

1. Preheat the oven to 177°C (350°F). Grease two 23-centimetre (9-inch) round cake pans with cooking spray, or a thin layer of neutral oil or softened butter, then line the bottoms with circles of parchment paper. Set aside.

2. Cream together the butter and sugar in the bowl of a stand mixer fitted with a paddle attachment. Start the mixer on low, until the ingredients are just combined, then increase to medium-high and mix, scraping down the sides of the bowl and the paddle with a rubber spatula about halfway through, for 8 to 10 minutes, until very light and fluffy.

3. With the mixer still going, add one of the eggs and let the mixer beat until fully incorporated. Repeat with the remaining eggs, then beat in the vanilla until combined.

4. Whisk together the salt, baking powder, and cake flour in a medium bowl. Reduce mixer speed to low, then add ⅓ of the flour mixture. Beat to combine, then add half the buttermilk. Beat to combine, then scrape down the paddle attachment and the sides and bottom of the bowl. Repeat the process with the remaining flour and buttermilk.

5. Split the cake batter equally between both cake pans, spreading evenly in each. Bake for 30 to 35 minutes, until a toothpick or cake tester inserted in the centre of the cake comes out with just a few moist crumbs clinging to it. Let cool in the pans for about 10 minutes, then turn out onto a wire cooling rack to cool completely, about 1 to 2 hours.

Recipe continued on next page

6. Beat together the butter and icing/powdered sugar in the bowl of a stand mixer fitted with a paddle attachment on low until just combined. Increase the speed to medium-high and beat, scraping down the sides of the bowl and paddle as needed, until smooth, light, and fluffy, about 10 minutes. Add the vanilla, salt, and cream and beat until smooth.

7. If the tops of the cakes are rounded, trim the rounded dome off with a large serrated knife to create a level surface. Place one layer of cake on a platter. Spread half of the frosting over the top, but not quite all the way to the edge (spreading the jam on top will help push it to the edge).

8. Spread the jam over the top of the frosting in an even layer. Place the second cake on top, then spread the remaining frosting over the top of the cake. Carefully push some of the frosting down the edge of the top layer of cake in an irregular swooping pattern. Slice and serve.

To make the Chocolate Cake:

Replace ½ cup of the cake flour with 42 grams (½ cup) cocoa powder, and 118 millilitres (½ cup) of the buttermilk with 118 millilitres (½ cup) hot coffee. At the start of the process, mix the cocoa powder with the hot coffee, let cool to room temperature, then whisk this mixture with the buttermilk. Proceed with the recipe as directed. For the frosting, melt 170 grams (1 cup) bittersweet chocolate chips (i.e., dark chocolate with at least 70% cocoa solids) in a small bowl in the microwave in 30-second bursts, stirring each time, until melted and smooth. Let cool to just above room temperature. Prepare the frosting as directed, then beat in the melted chocolate until smooth. Omit the strawberry jam and decorate as directed.

To make the Anniversary Cake:

Bake the cakes and prepare the frosting as directed. Transfer 2⅔ ounces (⅓ cup) of the frosting to a small bowl, then transfer ½ the remaining frosting to a medium bowl. Add 1½ teaspoons freeze-dried raspberry powder to the 2⅔ ounces (⅓ cup) reserved frosting and beat with a hand mixer until smooth. If needed, add 2 drops of pink gel food colouring to achieve a deeper pink colour. Add ½ teaspoon ube extract to the frosting reserved in the medium bowl and beat in with a hand mixer until smooth. Omit the strawberry jam, place the first layer of cake on a platter, and spread the ube-flavoured frosting over the top in an even layer. Place the second cake on top, then spread the reserved plain frosting over the top in an even layer. Transfer the raspberry frosting to a piping bag fitted with a star attachment. Pipe a ring of rosettes around the outer edge of the top of the cake. Scatter 1 tablespoon multicoloured sprinkles over the white part of the cake.

To make the Cake of Guidance:

Prepare the batter and frosting as directed. Divide the batter among two 12-cup muffin tins lined with paper cupcake cups, about 60 millilitres (¼ cup) of batter per cupcake. Bake at 177°C (350°F) for 20 to 22 minutes, or until a toothpick inserted into the middle of the cupcake comes out with a few moist crumbs clinging to it. Let the cupcakes cool in the pan for about 10 minutes, then transfer to a wire cooling rack to cool completely. Swap the strawberry jam for seedless raspberry jam and spread a thin layer on each cupcake. Transfer the frosting to a piping bag fitted with a large star tip. Pipe large rosettes on top of each cupcake, then top each rosette with a fresh raspberry. Arrange the cupcakes into a question mark.

CHEESECAKE / *No-Bake Cheesecake*

One of the most amazing parts of travelling to distant lands is the ability to sample novel flavours. Still, every now and then I find myself yearning for a taste of home, and that's when I often seek out the locals' version of cheesecake.

Whether flavoured with vanilla pods from the Kharazi Jungle, chocolate from the Grand Tree, or fresh strawberries from the fields of Falador or Ardougne, this creamy dessert instantly soothes my mind and readies me for another day of exploring.

This no-bake version is especially nice at the height of summer, when everyone wants to make use of their bounty of sun-ripened berries, yet no one wants to be stuck next to a hot range.

YIELD: *Serves 8 to 12* | PREP TIME: *20 minutes* | COOK TIME: *4 hours to chill* | DIFFICULTY: *Novice*

Equipment

Small saucepan, 23-centimetre (9-inch) tart pan with a removable bottom, stand mixer

Crust

8 ounces (2⅓ cups) digestive biscuits/graham crackers, finely crushed

8 tablespoons unsalted butter

½ teaspoon coarse sea/kosher salt

Filling

16 ounces cream cheese

100 grams (½ cup) granulated sugar

Juice and zest of 1 lemon

236 millilitres (1 cup) double/heavy cream

118 millilitres (½ cup) sour cream

1 tablespoon vanilla extract

60 millilitres (¼ cup) limoncello (optional)

To Serve

Seasonal berries, roughly chopped, for garnish

◆ *1 pile of bacon (chopped)*

1. Place the digestive biscuit/graham cracker crumbs in a medium bowl. Set aside. Heat the butter and salt together in a small saucepan over medium heat until melted. Cook, stirring and scraping constantly with a rubber spatula until the solids are golden brown. Fold into the crumbs until they're uniformly moistened.

2. Pour the crust mixture into a 23-centimetre (9-inch) tart pan with a removable bottom. Spread evenly with rubber spatula, press in with your hands, then use a flat-bottomed drinking glass or measuring cup to tightly compress the crust into the bottom and sides of the pan. Chill while you make the filling.

3. Beat the cream cheese, sugar, and lemon juice and zest together in the bowl of a stand mixer fitted with a paddle attachment on medium speed until smooth and fluffy. Add the cream and sour cream, mix until smooth, then increase the speed to high and beat until the volume is increased and the mixture holds stiff peaks, about 5 to 7 minutes. Reduce speed to medium and mix in the vanilla and limoncello (if using) until well combined.

4. Pour the filling into the prepared tart shell and swirl the top with a rubber spatula. Chill until set (at least 4 hours). Slice and serve with chopped seasonal berries.

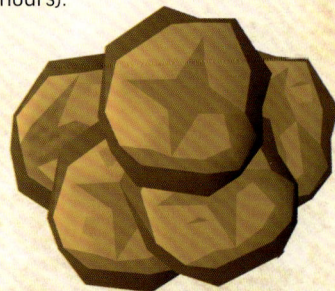

REDBERRY PIE / *Cherry Pie*

For the longest time, I could not uncover the reason why Redberry Pie was so popular among blacksmiths, especially those of the Imcando dwarves. Though redberries are undoubtedly delicious at the height of summer when they reach their peak ripeness, so too are many other fruits. I finally asked the smithy of Lumbridge castle why this peculiar penchant existed, and he taught me this workman's rhyme:

'Strike yer iron and shape it fine. While yellow or orange, wait to dine. Once the redberry glow begins to die, set to heat and eat your pie.'

YIELD: *Serves 6 to 8*　|　PREP TIME: *30 minutes*　|　COOK TIME: *1 hour*　|　DIFFICULTY: *Intermediate*

Equipment

Food processor, 23-centimetre (9-inch) pie dish/plate

Piecrust

300 grams (2½ cups) plain/all-purpose flour

16 tablespoons cold unsalted butter, cut into 1.25-centimetre (½-inch) cubes

2 tablespoons granulated sugar

½ teaspoon coarse sea/kosher salt

78 millilitres (⅓ cup) ice-cold water

Filling

1.13 kilograms (2½ pounds) pitted cherries (fresh or frozen—if using frozen, allow to thaw)

100 grams (½ cup) granulated sugar

28 grams (¼ cup) tapioca starch

¼ teaspoon coarse sea/kosher salt

2 teaspoons vanilla extract

¼ teaspoon almond extract

Juice and zest of 1 lime

1 large egg

1 tablespoon milk

1 tablespoon demerara/raw sugar

✦ *2 teaspoons ground guam*

1. Place the flour, butter, sugar, and salt in the bowl of a food processor. Pulse until the texture of wet sand, about 2 minutes. Tip the mixture into a large bowl and add the ice water. Mix with a wooden spoon or stiff rubber spatula until moistened through and no dry flour remains. Add an additional 1 to 2 table-spoons of cold water if the dough is too dry. Divide the dough in half, shape into two discs, and tightly wrap with cling film/plastic wrap. Chill for 1 hour.

2. Toss the cherries together in a large bowl with the sugar, tapioca starch, salt, vanilla, almond extract, and lime zest and juice. Let sit at room temperature until the crust is ready.

3. Heat the oven to 205°C (400°F) and place the oven rack in the lower-third position. Roll one of the discs of pie dough out to a circle about 6 millimetres (¼ inch) thick on a liberally floured work surface. Carefully transfer to a deep 23-centimetre (9-inch) pie plate, allowing the dough to fill the plate with at least 2.5 centimetres (1 inch) of overhang. Transfer to the fridge while you roll out the top crust. Repeat the rolling process with the remaining dough.

4. Transfer the filling to the dough-lined pie plate. Beat the egg and milk together in a small bowl. Brush the edges of the dough, then carefully transfer the top crust to the pie plate. Trim the overhang to about 1.25 centimetres (½ inch), then fold the overhang over itself and crimp to seal.

5. Slice two slits in the centre of the top crust to allow steam to escape. Brush the entire surface of the crust with egg wash and sprinkle with raw sugar. Place the pie plate on a baking sheet and bake for 45 minutes to 1 hour, until the crust is deep golden brown and the filling is bubbling. Allow to cool for about 15 to 20 minutes before serving.

KARAMJAN RUM WITH SLICED BANANAS

Bananas Foster

◆◀▸◆

Although ale and cider dominate the taverns and pubs of Misthalin, it is bottles of oft-smuggled Karamjan rum which feature in many of the kingdom's most sought-after desserts. Whether dressing up a plain cake with a sugar-rum glaze or paired with other exotic fruits to capture a taste of the tropics, this spirit can be readily found in most private and public kitchens.

Though the preparation of this dish may look intimidating due to the need to burn off the alcohol before it can be served, it is an easy technique to master with a little practice. Should you hold any reservations, feel free to wear your ice gloves for the first few attempts.

YIELD: *Serves 2* | PREP TIME: *5 minutes* | COOK TIME: *10 minutes* | DIFFICULTY: *Intermediate*

Equipment

25.5-centimetre (10-inch) stainless-steel frying pan/skillet

4 tablespoons unsalted butter

66 grams (1/3 cup) brown sugar

1 teaspoon cinnamon

½ teaspoon ground ginger

¼ teaspoon ground clove

2 ripe but still firm bananas, sliced into 1.25-centimetre-thick (½-inch-thick) coins

1 teaspoon vanilla extract

60 millilitres (¼ cup) spiced rum

Cinnamon ice cream, to serve

◆ *2 marinated jogre bones*

1. Heat the butter in a 25.5-centimetre (10-inch) stainless-steel skillet over medium-high heat on a gas stove until melted, then stir in the brown sugar, cinnamon, ginger, and clove. Cook, stirring constantly, until bubbling, thickened, and fragrant, about 3 minutes.

2. Add the bananas and cook, tossing occasionally, until lightly browned and caramelised, about 3 minutes.

3. Carefully add the vanilla and rum, then tip the pan forwards towards the flames to ignite the rum. Allow the flames to die down naturally while shaking and swirling the pan occasionally. If you don't have a gas range, remove from heat and use a long lighter to ignite the rum.

4. Scoop cinnamon ice cream into four bowls, then divide the bananas and sauce evenly between the bowls and serve immediately.

DWARVEN ROCK CAKE
Brown Sugar Cinnamon Rock Cakes

It is said dwarves love three things above all others: drinking, fishing, and gold. As I discovered during a recent trip to Catherby, intimate knowledge of these three can earn access to a fourth, more secretive passion—their love of baking.

As everyone knows, the quickest route west from Taverley is to go underneath White Wolf Mountain by way of the dwarven tunnels. It was while pausing to wet my whistle at their pub that I met a dwarf selling the most heavenly rock cakes. Scented with brown sugar and cinnamon, they were impossible to ignore, so I purchased one—only to nearly burn my bare hands on their incredible heat. After we shared a hearty laugh for my lack of ice gloves, the two of us got to talking about baking. Though he initially refused to divulge the secret to his recipe, some tall fish tales and my ability to produce mug after mug of Asgoldian ale as if by magic eventually won him over.

YIELD: *12 rock cakes* | PREP TIME: *15 minutes* | COOK TIME: *20 minutes* | DIFFICULTY: *Novice*

Equipment

46-by-33-centimetre (18-by-13-inch) baking tray/half-sheet pan, food processor

240 grams (2 cups) plain/all-purpose flour

100 grams (½ cup) dark brown sugar

1½ teaspoon baking powder

1½ teaspoon cinnamon

½ teaspoon coarse sea/kosher salt

8 tablespoons unsalted butter, cut into 2.5-centimetre (1-inch) pieces

80 grams (½ cup) mixed dried fruit, like raisins, currants, dried blueberries, and dried cherries

1 large egg

2 tablespoons whole milk

1 tablespoon vanilla extract

4 or 5 stems dwarf weed

1. Heat the oven to 177°C (350°F). Line a half-sheet pan with parchment paper.

2. Place the flour, dark brown sugar, baking powder, cinnamon, salt, and butter in the bowl of a food processor. Pulse until the mixture resembles the texture of wet sand.

3. Tip the contents of the food processor into a large bowl. Add the dried fruit and toss to distribute. Beat the egg, milk, and vanilla together in a small bowl, then add to the flour mixture. Stir together with a wooden spoon until a thick dough forms.

4. Use a ¼-cup measure or standard ice-cream scoop to measure out 12 rock cakes onto the prepared parchment. Bake for 17 to 20 minutes, until golden brown. Allow to cool in the pan for 5 minutes, then transfer to a wire cooling rack to cool completely.

FESTIVE GINGERBREAD GNOMES
Gingerbread Cookies

Whether you live along the snowy borders of Asgarnia and Kandarin, inhabit the tropical climates of Karamja, dwell within the sun-scorched lands of the Kharidian Desert, or wander the bucolic pasturelands of Misthalin, the winter holiday season usually means ingesting a stomach-busting number of festive gingerbread gnome cookies.

   Though no one knows exactly why these delectable cookies were first shaped like gnomes (some speculate it was a ploy to trick a band of ogres), the shape has become synonymous with Wintumber. This version, which is made for the children of Lumbridge every year, features a delightful royal icing to make the cookies even more special.

YIELD: *2 to 4 dozen, depending on cutters size* | **PREP TIME:** *20 minutes* | **COOK TIME:** *7 minutes* | **DIFFICULTY:** *Intermediate*

Equipment

Small saucepan, 46-by-33-centimetre (18-by-13-inch) baking tray/half-sheet pan, cookie cutters (see note)

Gingerbread Gnome Cookies

8 tablespoons unsalted butter

100 grams (½ cup) dark brown sugar

170 grams (½ cup) treacle/unsulphured molasses

¾ teaspoon coarse sea/kosher salt

2 teaspoons ground ginger

1½ teaspoons cinnamon

½ teaspoon fresh black pepper

¼ teaspoon ground clove

¼ teaspoon ground mace

1 large egg

¾ teaspoon baking powder

½ teaspoon bicarbonate/baking soda

240 grams (2 cups) plain/all-purpose flour

Ingredients continued on next page

1. Heat the butter in a small saucepan over medium heat until melted and foaming. Cook, stirring and scraping constantly with a rubber spatula, until the solids turn golden brown, about 5 to 8 minutes. Stir in the brown sugar and treacle/molasses until smooth.

2. Transfer the butter mixture to a medium bowl. Stir in the salt, ginger, cinnamon, pepper, clove, and mace until smooth. Beat in the egg until smooth.

3. Whisk together the baking powder, bicarbonate/baking soda, and flour in a small bowl. Stir into the butter mixture with a wooden spoon until a smooth, soft dough forms and no dry flour remains. Shape into a disc, wrap tightly with cling film/plastic wrap, and chill for at least 1 hour, until firm.

4. Preheat the oven to 177°C (350°F) and line a half-sheet pan with parchment paper. Unwrap the dough and transfer to a generously floured work surface. Roll with a floured rolling pin to a thickness of 6 millimetres (¼ inch). Use floured cookie cutters in your favourite shapes to punch out as many cookies as you can.

5. Transfer the cookies to the prepared sheet pan, leaving about 1.25 centimetres (½ inch) of space between each one (they won't spread much). Bake for 10 to 12 minutes, until firm and just beginning to brown at the edges. Let cool in the pan for a few minutes, then transfer to a wire cooling rack to cool completely.

Recipe continued on next page

Royal Icing

224 grams (2 cups) icing/powdered sugar

2 large egg whites

2 teaspoons vanilla extract

½ teaspoon coarse sea/kosher salt

1 to 2 tablespoons double/heavy cream

✦ *24 cut sapphires (for eyes)*

Gnome-shaped cookie cutters are available made-to-order from most modern general stores, but you can also get creative. Take a cutter shaped like an ice-cream cone and flip it upside down—the cone will be the hat. Pinch the edges of the ears to make them sharper, shape the tip of the hat to your liking, and add a small, cute nose on top. You can get creative with the icing, too. You could cover all of it in icing, cover just the hat, or use multiple colours of icing to decorate their hat, eyes, and mouths!

6. While the cookies bake, gather the scraps of dough and shape them into a disc. If the dough is quite soft, rewrap with cling film/plastic wrap and keep in the fridge while this batch of cookies bakes. Otherwise, reroll to a thickness of 6 millimetres (¼ inch) and repeat the cookie-cutting process. Repeat with the remaining dough until you've used it all.

7. Beat the icing sugar, egg whites, vanilla, and salt together in a medium bowl with a hand mixer until smooth and thick, about 5 to 7 minutes. Beat in 1 tablespoon cream until smooth, then check the consistency. It should be thick enough to hold its shape, but fluid enough to be easily moved with a small offset spatula. If it's too thick, add 1 tablespoon cream and beat until smooth.

8. From here, you can dip the tops of the cookies into the icing, let the excess drip off, then flip over and let set on a wire cooling rack (the setting process takes about 3 hours). Alternatively, you can transfer the icing to a piping bag fitted with a fine writing tip and decorate the cookies more intricately. And if you're feeling particularly glam, place two small sapphires or candied angelica on each cookie for dazzling gnome eyes. (But for the love of gods, do not eat the sapphires.)

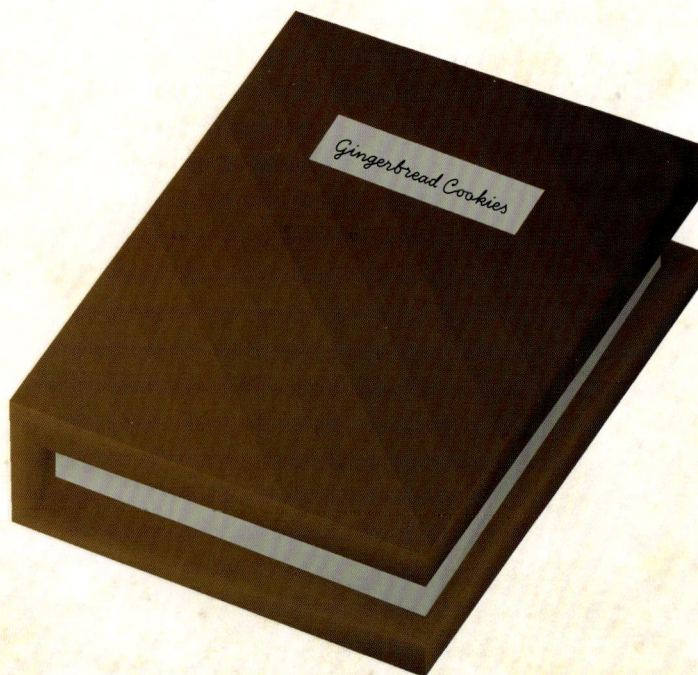

Gingerbread Cookies

CHOCCHIP CRUNCHIES / *Chocolate Chip Cookies*

To visit Ta Quir Priw is to know the serenity of nature . . . and the smell of fresh-baked breads and sweets carried upon the breeze. I remember fondly my first visit to the Grand Tree, and how delighted I was by the tree gnomes' careful preparation of their various Battas and world-famous Chocchip Crunchies.

Those delectable cookies are traditionally made with a variation of their base Gianne Dough which swaps out yeast for leavener before adding cold butter. This recipe simplifies the process further by softening the butter beforehand. As these rich cookies bake, it will fill your home with a sweet, cosy scent which warms any heart.

YIELD: *About 5 dozen* | PREP TIME: *15 minutes* | COOK TIME: *15 minutes* | DIFFICULTY: *Novice*

Equipment

46-by-33-centimetre (18-by-13-inch) baking tray/half-sheet pan, stand mixer

12 tablespoons unsalted butter, softened

150 grams (¾ cup) dark brown sugar

50 grams (¼ cup) granulated sugar

¾ teaspoon coarse sea/kosher salt

½ teaspoon bicarbonate/baking soda

1 large egg

1 tablespoon vanilla extract

150 grams (1¼ cups) plain/all-purpose flour

12 ounces dark chocolate chips (at least 70% cocoa solids)

✦ *2 shakes gnome spice*

1. Preheat the oven to 177°C (350°F). Line a half-sheet pan with parchment paper.

2. Cream together the butter, dark brown sugar, granulated sugar, salt, and bicarbonate/baking soda in the bowl of a stand mixer fitted with a paddle attachment. Beat on low for the first 1 minute, until the ingredients are moistened, then increase the speed to medium-high and mix until light and fluffy, about 7 to 9 minutes.

3. Beat in the egg and vanilla until fully incorporated, about 3 minutes. Reduce mixer speed to low, then add the flour. Mix until just combined, then add the chocolate chips and mix until evenly distributed.

4. Use a 1-tablespoon cookie scoop or 1-tablespoon measure to portion out 12 cookies. Space them evenly on the parchment-lined baking sheet (there will be a lot of space between each cookie, but they will spread as they bake). Bake for 12 to 15 minutes until deep golden brown and set.

5. Let cool in the pan for 5 minutes, then transfer to a wire cooling rack to cool completely. Repeat the scooping and baking process with the remaining dough.

HOLY BISCUITS / Sugar Cookies

The baking and consumption of Holy Biscuits is a peculiar yet beloved tradition across much of Gielinor. Created to mark the passage of special events and holidays, each is decorated with one of three holy symbols. The first is a yellow star evoking Saradomin, the god of order and wisdom. In eternal opposition is Zamorak, god of chaos, signified by red horns. Lastly is the god of balance, Guthix, whose chosen mark is a tear, root, or snake.

Although most revelers give very little stock to which biscuits they receive during festivities, some swear by the holy food's ability to grant them a glimpse into their future fortunes.

YIELD: *About 2 dozen* | **PREP TIME:** *15 minutes* | **COOK TIME:** *15 minutes* | **DIFFICULTY:** *Novice*

Equipment

Stand mixer, 46-by-33-centimetre (18-by-13-inch) baking tray/half-sheet pan

12 tablespoons unsalted butter, room temperature

150 grams (¾ cup) granulated sugar

1 teaspoon coarse sea/kosher salt

¼ teaspoon baking powder

¼ teaspoon bicarbonate/baking soda

1 tablespoon vanilla extract

1 large egg

300 grams (2½ cups) plain/all-purpose flour

Royal Icing

227 grams (2 cups) icing/powdered sugar

2 large egg whites

2 teaspoons vanilla extract

½ teaspoon coarse sea/kosher salt

1 to 2 tablespoons double/heavy cream

Ingredients continued on next page

1. Cream together the butter, sugar, salt, baking powder, bicarbonate/baking soda, and vanilla in the bowl of a stand mixer fitted with a paddle attachment. Start the mixer on low until the sugar is moistened, then increase the speed to medium-high and mix until light and fluffy, about 5 to 7 minutes.

2. Add the egg and beat until fully incorporated and smooth, about 3 minutes. Reduce the mixer speed to low and add the flour. Mix until no dry streaks of flour remain. Shape the dough into a disc, wrap tightly with cling film/plastic wrap, and chill for 30 minutes.

3. Preheat the oven to 177°C (350°F). Line a half-sheet pan with a sheet of parchment paper.

4. Place the dough on a floured work surface. Roll to a thickness of 6 millimetres (¼ inch). Use a floured 5-centimetre (2-inch) round cookie cutter to cut out as many cookies as you can. Transfer to the prepared baking sheet, leaving about 1.25 centimetres (½ inch) of space between each cookie (they won't spread very much). Bake for 13 to 15 minutes until just turning pale gold around the edges. Let the cookies cool on the sheet for 10 minutes, then transfer to a wire cooling rack to cool completely.

5. Gather up the scraps of dough, shape them into a disc, then repeat the rolling, cutting, and baking process until all of the dough is used.

Recipe continued on next page

Decoration

Yellow petal powder

Green petal powder

Red petal powder

3 tablespoons vodka or other clear or lightly coloured liquor or liqueur, or flavour extracts, such as vanilla, mint, etc.

✦ *3 leaves grimy marrentill*

Use vodka to create the decoration if you don't want to add any more flavour to the cookies. Otherwise, use flavoured liqueurs to add a hint of something extra.

Petal and lustre powders are essentially dry, powdered food colouring, which you can then turn into a reliable, opaque paint for your cookies using liqueur or clear flavour extracts (the latter will give the cookies an extra pop of flavour!). This is preferable to liquid food colouring, because you only need a small amount of powder to create an opaque paint

When creating Holy Biscuits, feel free to depict the symbol of the god who matches your allegiance! To get clean lines, you may choose to order some cake tracers from the most modern of general stores, or utilise illusion spells to project the images onto the biscuit.

---

6. Beat the icing/powdered sugar, egg whites, vanilla, and salt together in a medium bowl with a hand mixer until smooth and thick, about 5 to 7 minutes. Beat in 1 tablespoon cream until smooth, then check the consistency. It should be thick enough to hold its shape but fluid enough to be easily moved with a small offset spatula. If it's too thick, add 1 tablespoon cream and beat until smooth.

7. Dip the tops of the cooled cookies into the icing. Use an offset spatula to wipe off the excess and spread the icing to the edges of the cookies. Transfer to a wire cooling rack and let sit at room temperature until the icing sets, at least 6 hours.

8. Add 1 tablespoon vodka each to three small bowls. Mix yellow petal powder into one of the bowls, a pinch at a time, until it turns opaque. Repeat with the second bowl and green petal powder, and the third bowl with red petal powder. Use small decorating brushes to paint Saradomin's symbol in yellow on ⅓ of the cookies, Guthix's green root symbol on ⅓ of the cookies, and Zamorak's red horn symbol on the remaining ⅓. Let the cookies dry for at least 1 hour before storing in an airtight container at room temperature.

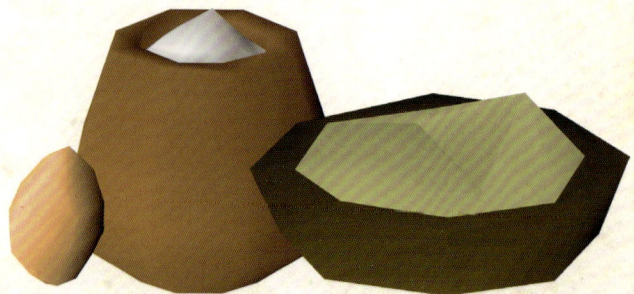

PURPLE SWEETS / *Ube Caramels*

When the holidays approach, it should come as no surprise that, as a chef, my mind is on all the delicious foods which make the season so special. One iconic treat makes its yearly appearance just in time for Hallowe'en: the gooey, sticky treat known as Purple Sweets.

With their tidy wrappers and compact size, these sweets are a favourite of travellers looking to conserve bag space but still have a ready source of energy. I once even met a warrior who claimed they made him invincible and would allow him to slay the legendary monster TzTok-Jad. Unfortunately, the man has never come back to tell me the story, so I'd take his boast with a grain of sea salt.

YIELD: *About 60 caramels* | PREP TIME: *15 minutes* | COOK TIME: *2 hours, plus 4 to 5 hours cooling* | DIFFICULTY: *Master*

Equipment

23-by-33-centimetre (9-by-13-inch) baking tray/quarter-sheet pan, 3.8-litre (4-quart) Dutch oven. sugar/candy thermometer

16 tablespoons unsalted butter, plus more for the pan

354 millilitres (1½ cups) double/ heavy cream

118 millilitres (½ cup) whole milk

236 millilitres (1 cup) golden/light corn syrup

500 grams (2½ cups) granulated sugar

100 grams (½ cup) light brown sugar, lightly packed

¾ teaspoon coarse sea/kosher salt

2 tablespoons vanilla extract

1½ teaspoon ube extract

✦ *2 sprigs clean cadantine*

1. Grease a quarter-sheet pan (about 23-by-33 centimetres or 9-by-13 inches) with butter. Set aside.

2. Heat the butter, cream, whole milk, golden syrup, granulated sugar, brown sugar, and salt in a 3.8-litre (4-quart) Dutch oven over medium-low heat until the butter melts.

3. Attach a sugar/candy thermometer to the side of the Dutch oven. Cook, stirring constantly, until the thermometer registers 120°C (250°F), about 2 hours.

4. Remove from heat and stir in the vanilla and ube extracts. Stir vigorously to incorporate—the mixture will bubble up quickly, then subside. Stir until the colour is uniformly purple.

5. Pour the caramel into the prepared quarter-sheet pan, but do not scrape out the contents of the Dutch oven (the caramel bits clinging to the bottom of the Dutch oven are totally edible once cooled but may give an irregular texture to the final batch—best to scrape into a separate bowl to snack on while you let the prettier, more popular caramels cool). Let cool on the counter for 1 hour, then cover tightly with foil and chill until the caramel is set and firm, 3 to 4 hours.

6. Uncover the caramels and invert the pan over a cutting board. Set a pan of hot water on top of the quarter-sheet pan to help melt the butter and loosen the caramels from the pan—listen for a thud after a few minutes. If the caramels don't dislodge themselves on their own, give the pan a sharp tap to release them.

7. Use a very sharp knife or metal bench scraper to cut the caramels into 2.5-centimetre (1-inch) cubes. Wrap each with waxed paper. If desired, wrap with purple-coloured candy/sweet wrappers (waxed or foil will work). Store in an airtight container for a few weeks. Caramels can be chilled or frozen for months.

BREADS

KING NARNODE SHAREEN

I know what you're going to say, so you can save your breath—there is most definitely a gnome monarch sitting at the duke's table. Oh, that's not what you were going to say? Well, then, spit it out and be quick about it.

Why are there not two gnome monarchs sitting at the table, you ask? I'm impressed by your surprising grasp of the gnomish monarchical structure, but you should be grateful to have one gnome in the hand rather than lament two in the bush, or tree, as it were.

Although rescuing the shortest royalty in the room may seem easy at first, your brief stint slinging grub for the Gnome Restaurant is not going to help you here. King Narnode Shareen may be a wise and just ruler, but he's notoriously picky about what passes for regal-worthy Batta. My suggestion: Start with fruits or onions, add a nutty cheese, pile it high on a pillowy round of Gianne Dough, then bake it to perfection. Satisfy the King's carb craving, and we'll be that much closer to defeating the Culinaromancer for good.

GIANNE DOUGH / *Basic Bread Dough*

For such a diminutive group, the gnomes have certainly made an outsized contribution to the culinary landscape of Gielinor. Though most known for their spice and designer cocktails, the gnomes of the Grand Tree are also excellent bakers of bread. What follows is the highly versatile dough used in their most popular gluten-based dishes.

YIELD: *4 dough balls* | PREP TIME: *15 minutes, plus 13 hours resting time* | COOK TIME: *N/A* | DIFFICULTY: *Novice*

480 grams (4 cups) bread flour

1 tablespoon coarse sea/kosher salt

2 teaspoons instant yeast

354 millilitres (1½ cups) water, room temperature

✦ *3 small chewy toads*

1. Whisk together the flour, salt, and yeast in a large bowl. Create a well in the centre and pour in the water. Use your hands to stir the ingredients together to create a thick, shaggy dough with no streaks of dry flour.

2. Cover the bowl and let sit at room temperature for 12 hours. Use your hand to separate the dough from the sides of the bowl. Starting at the 12-o'clock position, grip the dough and fold it in on itself. Turn the bowl 90 degrees and repeat. Repeat this process two more times. Cover the bowl and let the dough rise for an additional hour.

3. Divide the dough into 4 equal pieces, then proceed to your desired recipe, or store in lightly oiled 473-millilitre (1-pint) lidded containers in the fridge for up to 6 days. Note that the dough will continue to slowly ferment and develop flavour in the fridge, so the longer you wait, the more flavourful your final product will be. If you chill the dough, you will need to let it sit in the covered, oiled container at room temperature for 2 hours before proceeding with any of the following recipes.

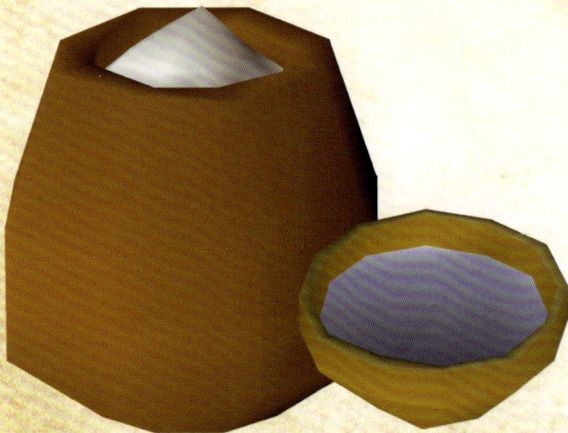

PITTA BREAD / *Pita*

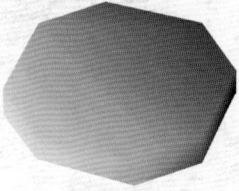

When most imagine the cities of the Kharidian Desert, they conjure thoughts of heat, sand, and extreme thirst. For me, however, it is the aroma of sizzling ugthanki meat set into rounds of fresh-baked dough topped with spicy sauce which fills my mind.

For as popular as kebabs are, I am often surprised to find that young chefs avoid making their own Pitta Bread until much later in their culinary journeys. We do use the oven, so if one can successfully make a loaf of bread, then they already have all the skill required to make this essential vessel for kebab meat.

YIELD: *8 pita* | PREP TIME: *2 hours* | COOK TIME: *5 minutes* | DIFFICULTY: *Intermediate*

Equipment

Stand mixer, pizza stone or 46-by-33-centimetre (18-by-13-inch) baking tray/half-sheet pan

2 teaspoons active dry yeast

1½ teaspoons granulated sugar

236 millilitres (1 cup) water, lukewarm

270 grams (2¼ cups) plain/all-purpose flour

60 grams (½ cup) wholemeal/whole wheat flour

1½ teaspoons coarse sea/kosher salt

3 tablespoons olive oil, plus more for bowl

Reindeer kebab meat (if in season)

To reheat the pitas, heat a cast-iron skillet over high heat, then warm the pitas in the dry skillet for 1 minute on each side. Serve warm.

1. Whisk the yeast, sugar, and water together in a small bowl. Let sit for 5 to 10 minutes, or until the yeast is foamy.

2. Add the flours, salt, and olive oil to the bowl of a stand mixer fitted with the dough hook attachment. Mix on low to combine the ingredients, about 2 minutes.

3. With the mixer running, add the yeast mixture and continue mixing until a shaggy dough forms, about 3 minutes. Increase the speed to medium and mix until the dough is smooth and elastic, about 7 to 10 minutes longer.

4. Coat the inside of a large bowl with olive oil, then transfer the dough to the oiled bowl. Drizzle with more olive oil and turn to coat. Cover with cling film/plastic wrap or a clean, damp kitchen towel and let rise in a warm place until quite puffy, about 1 hour.

5. Preheat the oven to 260°C (500°F) with the rack set at the lowest position. Place a pizza stone on the rack (or an inverted, heavy-duty baking sheet). Turn the dough out onto a lightly oiled work surface and divide into 8 equal portions.

6. Working with one piece of dough at a time, and keeping the remaining dough balls covered with a damp kitchen towel, roll the dough out to 20-centimetre (8-inch) circles about 3 millimetres (⅛ inch) thick. Once the dough has all been rolled out, cover with a damp kitchen towel and let rest for about 30 minutes, until puffed (Leave the oven on while the dough rests; the pizza stone or inverted pan needs to get very hot.)

7. Take two circles of dough and place them on the preheated pizza stone (or baking sheet). Bake for 3 to 5 minutes, until puffed and golden. Stack the pitas and wrap them in a clean kitchen towel (this will help keep them soft). Repeat the process with the remaining pitas. Store any extras in an airtight container for up to 3 days.

BATTA / *Ciabatta, Three Ways*

When one first hears the description of a gnome batta, it may conjure thoughts of a pizza—yet the two have several distinct differences. Although both often start with a ball of Gianne Dough, they quickly diverge in thickness and toppings.

To make a proper batta, dough must be stretched into a pan and then left to rise until pillowy. Savoury or sweet toppings are next added to create a thick Batta which is both soft and flavourful. One regional favourite is Worm Batta, so named for the nutritious king worms sprinkled generously on top—but I've uncovered two more variations and have noted them all here.

YIELD: *Serves 4* | PREP TIME: *2 hours* | COOK TIME: *20 minutes* | DIFFICULTY: *Intermediate*

Equipment

46-by-33-centimetre (18-by-13-inch) baking tray/half-sheet pan

1 batch Gianne Dough (page 112)
Plain/all-purpose flour, for dusting
6 ice cubes
◆ *4 stems clean toadflax*

Worm Batta

1 large onion or 2 medium onions

8 teaspoons grated Parmesan cheese

113 grams (1 cup) shredded mozzarella cheese

Cheese+Tom Batta

113 grams (1 cup) shredded mozzarella cheese

4 tablespoons finely chopped sun-dried tomatoes

Olive oil, for topping

Flaked sea salt, for topping

Basil leaves, finely sliced, for topping

Ingredients continued on next page

1. Preheat the oven to 233°C (450°F) and place the oven rack in the centre position. Place a metal baking pan in the bottom of the oven. Line a half-sheet pan with greaseproof/parchment paper.

2. Turn one ball of dough out onto a floured work surface. Shape the dough into a ball by cupping your hands on either side of the dough and gently pulling the top of the dough towards the bottom while spinning the dough along the work surface. Repeat until the top of the dough looks slightly taut.

3. Stretch the dough into a 13-centimetre-long (5-inch-long) log. Dust the top with flour, then transfer to the prepared parchment paper. Repeat with the remaining balls of dough, leaving enough room between them to expand. Cover with a clean kitchen towel and let rise in a warm place for 60 to 90 minutes, until quite puffed and nearly doubled in size.

4. Place the pan on the centre rack, then quickly toss the ice cubes into the pan at the bottom of the oven and close the oven door. This will create steam and help give the bread a nice crust. Bake for 18 to 20 minutes, until deep golden.

Recipe continued on next page

Fruit Batta

55 grams (⅓ cup) pineapple chunks

55 grams (⅓ cup) cara cara or blood orange slices, rinds and membranes removed, roughly chopped

Zest of ½ lime

38 grams (⅓ cup) aged Gouda cheese

1 teaspoon granulated sugar

¼ teaspoon cinnamon

1 pinch cardamom

Basil leaves, finely sliced, for topping

To make the Worm Batta:

Cut the onions into 1.25-centimetre (½-inch) slices and cook over medium-low heat with 2 tablespoons of oil and ¼ teaspoon kosher salt for about 1 hour in a heavy-bottomed saucepan, stirring frequently. As you cook the onions, you may notice brown bits sticking to the bottom of the pan—add a splash of water as needed, scrape these up with a wooden spoon, and fold into the onions as you stir. Repeat as needed until the onions are deeply browned, soft, and caramelised. Divide the carmelised onions, Parmesan cheese, and mozzarella evenly amongst each roll, topping while the rolls are still hot. Return to the oven for 3 to 5 minutes until the cheese is melted. Serve warm or at room temperature. Keep stored in an airtight container and eat within 3 days.

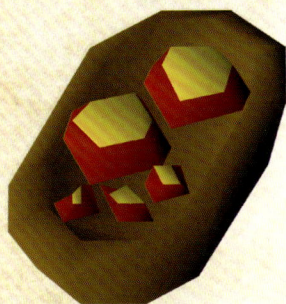

To make the Cheese+Tom Batta:

Top each hot roll, dividing the mozzarella and sun-dried tomatoes evenly amongst each roll and finishing with a drizzle of olive oil and a pinch of flaky sea salt. Return to the oven for 3 to 5 minutes until the cheese is melted. Top with finely sliced basil leaves. Serve warm or at room temperature. Keep stored in an airtight container and eat within 3 days.

To make the Fruit Batta:

Finely chop the pineapple chunks and cara cara orange slices. Mix the pineapple and orange together in a small bowl with the aged Gouda cheese, lime zest, granulated sugar, cinnamon, and cardamom. Divide this mixture over the four rolls, then return to the oven for 3 to 5 minutes, until the cheese is melted. Top with finely sliced basil leaves. Serve warm or at room temperature. Keep stored in an airtight container and eat within 3 days.

PIZZA, THREE WAYS

◆ ◆

To be recognised as an accredited chef, all apprentices must first prove their skills to the Cooks' Guild in the city of Varrock. Here, aspiring culinary artists are tasked to produce a variety of meals, including a pizza of their choosing which can feed exactly fifty-two hungry patrons.

Where I thought I was being bold by topping my pizza with fire-roasted jubbly, another student ventured to tackle the mythical banana pizza, an infamous dare made between apprentices during our many years of training. Although it was perhaps not for everyone's palate, the unique combination of sliced bananas, nuts, curry leaves, and cooked chicken gained quite a loyal following and soundly earned my fellow student her chef's hat. I have yet to re-create her masterpiece, but I've recorded three beloved varieties of pizza below.

YIELD: *Four 10-inch pizzas* | PREP TIME: *15 minutes* | COOK TIME: *15 minutes* | DIFFICULTY: *Intermediate*

Equipment

Pizza stone or 46-by-33-centimetre (18-by-13-inch) baking tray/half-sheet pan, pizza peel

1 batch Gianne Dough (page 112)

Cornmeal or semolina flour, for sprinkling

236 millilitres (1 cup) pizza sauce, divided

227 grams (2 cups) shredded mozzarella cheese, divided

✦ *5 buds clean snapdragon*

Ingredients continued on next page

1. Preheat the oven to 260℃ (500°F) and place the oven rack in the lower-third position. Place a pizza stone on the oven rack and let preheat for at least 30 minutes before baking your pizzas. If you don't have a pizza stone, an inverted half-sheet pan will work here.

2. Turn one of the four balls of dough out onto a floured work surface. Stretch into a roughly 10-to-12-inch circle by first shaping the dough into a disc. Make two loose fists and let the dough drape over one fist, then toss it from fist to fist, letting gravity do most of the work. You can also gently grip the edges of the circle, let the dough hang vertically, and slowly spin the dough, again letting gravity do the work. Once the dough is roughly the size you want it, lay on the floured work surface and gently stretch it the rest of the way.

3. Generously sprinkle cornmeal or semolina flour all over a pizza peel (if you don't have one, an inverted half-sheet pan will do the trick). Lay the stretched dough on the pizza peel and, working quickly, top with ¼ of the pizza sauce and ¼ of the mozzarella cheese. If you're making a speciality pizza, add additional toppings (see next page).

4. Slide the pizza onto the pizza stone, then bake for 12 to 15 minutes, until the dough is puffed and golden and the cheese is melted and bubbling. Repeat the shaping-and-baking process with the remaining dough balls.

Recipe continued on next page

Meat Pizza

A few handfuls meat of choice, such as pepperoni slices, cooked sausage, Cooked Jubbly (page 67), or Cooked Meat (page 68), divided

A few handfuls vegetables of choice, such as chopped roasted red bell peppers, Fried Mushrooms (page 51), finely chopped brown/yellow onions, or mixed bell peppers, divided

Crumbled cotija cheese, for topping (optional)

Pineapple Pizza

8 to 12 tablespoons finely chopped pineapple chunks

4 tablespoons finely chopped roasted red bell peppers

1 roughly chopped slice of mortadella

Anchovy Pizza

24 to 32 anchovy fillets

To make the Meat Pizza:

Top each pizza with sauce and cheese as directed, then add an even amount of the cooked meat and vegetables. The Fire-Roasted Chicken pairs well with roasted red bell peppers or Sautéed Wild Mushrooms. Carne Asada is delicious with yellow onion, mixed bell peppers, and cotija cheese. Whatever combo you use, limit yourself (if you can!) on the toppings to keep from overloading the pizza.

To make the Pineapple Pizza:

Top each pizza with sauce and cheese as directed, then add the pineapple chunks, roasted red bell peppers, and mortadella. Bake as directed.

To make the Anchovy Pizza:

Top each pizza with sauce and cheese as directed, then add 6 to 8 anchovy fillets to each, lining them up like the spokes on a bike wheel. Bake as directed.

In place of the cotija cheese, you could use Parmesan or Romano cheese, which add a nice aged, salty flavour to the pizza. The pizza will already have plenty of mozzarella, though, so feel free to omit entirely!

GNOMEBOWLS / *Bread Bowls*

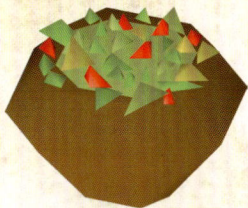

Vegetable dishes were quite rare and seen as a great luxury in traditional gnome cooking, since for most of their history, growing vegetables was a far more labour-intensive process than hunting toads and worms. This means that the first gnomebowls were likely filled with meat-heavy stews and broths, such as the beloved Tangled Toads' Legs created by gnome chef Deelie to commemorate the very first Healthorg the Great Day.

These days, gnomebowls can be found in pubs and taverns throughout Gielinor, serving all forms of local fare, including many of the soups and stews featured in this very book.

YIELD: *4 bread bowls* | PREP TIME: *2 hours* | COOK TIME: *20 minutes* | DIFFICULTY: *Intermediate*

Equipment

46-by-33-centimetre (18-by-13-inch) baking tray/half-sheet pan

1 batch Gianne Dough (page 112)
Olive oil, for greasing
Flaky sea salt, for sprinkling
◆ *2 handfuls wiggling king worms*

1. Preheat the oven to 233°C (450°F) and place the oven rack in the centre position. Line a half-sheet pan with parchment paper.

2. Turn out one of the dough balls onto an unfloured work surface. With oiled hands, shape the dough into a tight ball by gently gripping the sides with your hands cupped and spinning the dough in a tight circle until the top is quite taut and springy. Coat with oil and place on the prepared sheet pan. Repeat with the remaining balls of dough, spacing them evenly on the sheet pan.

3. Cover the shaped dough balls with an oiled sheet of cling film/plastic wrap and let rise in a warm place for 60 to 90 minutes, until quite puffed and nearly doubled in size. Sprinkle with flaky sea salt and bake for 17 to 20 minutes, until deep golden. Transfer to a wire rack to cool completely.

4. Pierce the top of the bread with a sharp serrated knife, inserting the knife about halfway through the bread at an angle. Carve out a circle, keeping the knife at that angle, to remove a cone of bread and create a bowl. Place on a plate and fill with any of the soups or stews in this book (page 20).

DRINKS

DUKE HORACIO

If you know anything about Duke Horacio, it's that he greatly values the safety and prosperity of all life on Gielinor. If you know a second thing about him, it's that his guest list often reflects the same rich diversity. No, I won't keep telling you 'Duke facts'; go and read his autobiography if you're so inclined. Right now, we have a world to save.

As anyone who has attended the duke's parties will attest, a defining feature of his shindigs is a brilliant signature cocktail which helps to ease conversation amongst his various guests. What, you've never been invited before? Not even after slaying that dragon or helping forge relations with the Dorgeshuun? You didn't even get a seat after rounding up all of those monkeys during the duke's birthday? If I may say so, it might be time to fire your PR agent.

Regardless of your social hang-ups, your final task will be to re-create the beverage at the heart of Lumbridge Castle's infamous drinking game, Duke's Cup. Yes, I know it's normally called King's Cup, but with so many kings in attendance, we won't know whose drink is whose. Speaking of which, be sure to make enough for everyone because the Culinaromancer's defeat is but one short, green sip away.

BLURBERRY SPECIAL / *Lemon Drop*

◀◆▶

All the study in the world can never replace the value of real-world experience. Such is especially the case when mastering mixology, where the alchemy of flavours can seem ever-changing. In my kingdom, that means making an annual pilgrimage to the Grand Tree to see what fantastical new cocktails have been invented at Blurberry's Bar, while also savouring tried-and-true favourites—like this namesake gem.

YIELD: *1 cocktail* | PREP TIME: *5 minutes* | COOK TIME: *N/A* | DIFFICULTY: *Novice*

Granulated sugar, for coating the rim

Lemon wedge, for coating the rim

60 millilitres (2 ounces) vodka

45 millilitres (1½ ounces) limoncello

30 millilitres (1 ounce) fresh-squeezed lemon juice

1 thin lemon slice

◆ *4 equa leaves*

1. Pour an even layer of sugar on the bottom of a small plate. Rub the lemon wedge along the rim of your cocktail glass, then dip the rim in the sugar to coat it. Set aside.

2. Pour the vodka, limoncello, and lemon juice into a cocktail shaker full of ice. Shake well, then strain into the cocktail glass. Garnish with the thin lemon slice.

If you want to try another fun garnish, take a 5-centimetre-long (2-inch-long), thin strip of lemon peel and twist it around so it curls cutely out of the glass.

ASGARNIAN ALE

Next in our imbibing tour is our very own local favourite—Asgarnian Ale. With its malt-focused sweetness, generous head, and golden colour, it's no wonder why it is the beer of choice throughout Gielinor. With only two primary breweries, located in Falador and Burthorpe, it typically falls to alewives and homebrewers to fill the huge demand, especially in rural areas.

Brewing is a specialised, centuries-old craft, and the instructions for it would fill another one of the Lumbridge chef's massive tomes. But because there will be enthusiasts among you, we've noted the ingredients needed for this special Asgarnian Ale recipe, fit for any king's table.

YIELD: *about 21 litres or 5½ gallons (26.5 litres or 7 gallons preboil)* | **RECIPE TYPE:** *All-grain*

3.6 kilograms (8 pounds) Maris Otter pale malt

(2.5 kilograms or 5½ pounds Golden Light dry malt extract if using extract)

900 grams (2 pounds) Honey Malt

15 millilitres (½ ounce) Target hop pellets (60 min)

15 millilitres (½ ounce) Northern Brewer hop pellets (60 min)

15 millilitres (½ ounce) East Kent Goldings hop pellets (15 min)

60 millilitres (2 ounces) Fuggle hop pellets (flameout)

1 teaspoon Irish moss or 1 tablet Whirlfloc (whirlpool)

London/English ale yeast (liquid or dry)

Beer Profile

Original Gravity: 1.057

Final Gravity: 1.014

ABV: 5.6%

IBU: 39

SRM: 9-10

✦ *1 gold coin per glass*

Once you have a glass of Asgarnian Ale, you can make the renowned Asgoldian Ale by stirring in ⅛ teaspoon gold lustre dust per 12 ounces of beer. Don't forget the gold coin!

POISON CHALICE / *Green Russian*

Culinary genius is not the sole domain of the professionally trained, and this cocktail always serves to remind me of that humbling fact. The creator of this recipe was a dwarven miner by the name of Stankers, whose job was to maintain the coal trucks west of Seers' Village. Showing our group true hospitability after our carriage broke down, Stankers offered us this mysterious brew while we awaited the village wainwright. Though not everyone was unanimous in their enjoyment or description, I was quite delighted by its slight yet inventive hint of apricot and requested the recipe.

| YIELD: *1 cocktail* | PREP TIME: *5 minutes* | COOK TIME: *N/A* | DIFFICULTY: *Novice* |

1 teaspoon matcha powder

1½ teaspoons granulated sugar

2 tablespoons boiling water

60 millilitres (2 ounces) vanilla vodka

30 millilitres (1 ounce) Midori

15 millilitres (1/2 ounce) apricot liqueur

30 millilitres (1 ounce) double/heavy cream

5 leaves clean tarromin and ashes

1. Whisk the matcha and sugar together in a small bowl until uniform with no lumps. Whisking constantly and vigorously, add the boiling water and continue whisking until smooth and the matcha and sugar have dissolved. Set aside to cool.

2. Pour the vodka, Midori, apricot liqueur, and matcha mixture into a shaker full of ice. Shake well and strain over a glass (or chalice) of ice. Top with the cream, carefully pouring it over the back of a spoon to avoid it sinking, and serve.

The Poison Chalice is a mysterious cocktail which may create strange side effects when imbibed. Consult the table if a strange sensation washes over you!

FEELING	EFFECTS
You feel a little better.	Your body may be weakened today, but you'll have a burst of creativity.
It has a slight taste of apricot.	No effect—but how refreshing!
You feel a little strange.	While your body reacts strangely, your mind and creativity benefit from the oddity.
It restores some life points.	You'll have a burst of vitality and strength today. Use it well.
You feel a lot better.	You're sharper now in both body and mind.
Wow! That was amazing! You feel really invigorated.	Strength and cunning are both yours to wield today. Take advantage!
That tasted a bit dodgy. You feel a bit ill.	You may find your faculties weakened—go have a lie-down, you'll feel better.
That tasted very dodgy. You feel very ill.	Oof. Not sure you're going to get anything at all done today.

MATURE CIDER / *Hot Mulled Cider*

Right as the first chilly evenings of autumn begin to displace the warmth of summer, I find myself yearning for a warm mug of cider from the dwarven city of Keldagrim. Though mature cider is delicious all on its own, this version incorporates the harvest flavours of mulling spices and cinnamon to get you in the mood for all the apple pies which will be baked in the coming months.

YIELD: *1 cocktail* | PREP TIME: *5 minutes* | COOK TIME: *N/A* | DIFFICULTY: *Novice*

Equipment

Large Dutch oven or slow cooker, large stainless-steel frying pan/skillet

1.89 litres (½ gallon) apple cider

12 cloves

4 cardamom pods, cracked

5 cinnamon sticks, divided

2 star anise pods

1 teaspoon coriander seeds

1 lemon, sliced into 1.25-centimetre (½-inch) slices

One 5-centimetre (2-inch) knob of ginger, sliced

2 tablespoons maple syrup

236 millilitres (1 cup) bourbon, whiskey, or dark rum

✦ *2 buckets apple mush*

1. Pour the apple cider into a large Dutch oven and bring to a bare simmer over medium-low heat.

2. As the cider warms, toast the cloves, cardamom pods, 4 cinnamon sticks, star anise pods, and coriander seeds over medium-high heat in a large stainless-steel skillet, tossing constantly, until fragrant and toasty, about 3 to 5 minutes.

3. Add the toasted spices, along with the lemon and ginger, to the cider. Let sit, barely simmering (the pot shouldn't bubble at all, just gently steam), for 4 hours.

4. Remove from heat and stir in the maple syrup and the spirit of your choice. Serve in mugs, garnished with the last cinnamon stick.

To prepare this recipe in a slow cooker, set the slow cooker to high, pour in the cider, then proceed with the recipe as directed. If you notice the cider bubbling at any point, reduce the heat to low.

CHOCOLATE SATURDAY / *Mocha Martini*

This delightful cocktail comes from my good friend and master chef, Aluft Gianne, who owns the aptly named Gnome Restaurant located on one of the many floors of the Grand Tree. A true visionary in our field, it was Aluft who taught me to be bolder in my ingredient pairings and to not fear failure, because even a bad idea will always teach us something.

YIELD: *1 cocktail* | PREP TIME: *5 minutes* | COOK TIME: *N/A* | DIFFICULTY: *Novice*

- 45 millilitres (1½ ounces) vanilla vodka
- 30 millilitres (1 ounce) coffee liqueur
- 30 millilitres (1 ounce) chocolate crème liqueur
- 1 shot espresso
- 15 millilitres (½ ounce) vanilla syrup
- ◆ *7 sharp blades snape grass*

1. Pour the vanilla vodka, coffee liqueur, chocolate crème liqueur, espresso, and vanilla syrup into a cocktail shaker full of ice. Shake well, then strain into a martini glass.

SHORT GREEN GUY / *Midori Sour*

It is no secret that adventuring allies make everything better. Yet when you add cocktails, what often results is a rousing minigame of King's Cup. Show off your Herblore mettle by making everyone at the table this rule-inspired beverage.

YIELD: *1 cocktail* | PREP TIME: *5 minutes* | COOK TIME: *N/A* | DIFFICULTY: *Novice*

60 millilitres (2 ounces) Midori

15 millilitres (½ ounce) vodka

15 millilitres (½ ounce) fresh lemon juice

15 millilitres (½ ounce) fresh lime juice

Club soda, for topping

Lime, for garnish

◆ *More equa leaves*

1. Pour the Midori, vodka, lemon juice, and lime juice into a shaker full of ice. Shake well, then strain over a collins glass full of ice.

2. Top with club soda and garnish with a thinly sliced lime.

This drink is traditionally made with a maraschino cherry—feel free to substitute the lime slice or, if you're feeling fun, add both!

QUEST CERTIFICATE

CONGRATULATIONS!

You have defeated the Culinaromancer for good!
You are renown throughout Gielinor for
your good deeds!

IRL INGREDIENTS GUIDE

Achiote paste: Used in Mexican, Central American, and South American cuisine, this premade paste is made from annatto seeds and a blend of spices, typically including cumin, garlic, oregano, ground coriander, and others. It can be found in many supermarkets, Latin American markets, and online.

Bird's eye chillis: These tiny chillis are native to Mexico but are commonly used in many Asian cuisines. They're sometimes called Thai bird's eye chillis or Thai red chillis and have a fruity, peppery flavour. Their heat level lies somewhere between jalapeños and habaneros, and they can be found in many grocery stores and Asian markets. They can also be found dried online. If you have trouble sourcing them, substitute with serrano chillis or dried cayenne powder. Depending on where you live, they may instead be spelled "chiles" or "chilies"!

Galangal: This rhizome is related to ginger and is used in many traditional Southeast Asian cuisines. Although similar in appearance to ginger, with some similar flavour notes, it's a bit more citrusy and piney. It can be found in some grocery stores and Asian markets but can also be found dried and powdered online. You can use ginger in its place, but if it doesn't have citrus notes you're looking for, add a bit of lime zest.

Ghee: Ghee is butter which has been cooked at a low temperature until the milk solids have browned slightly. The milk solids are then discarded, leaving a clarified butter with a grassy, nutty taste. It is commonly used in Indian cuisine and Ayurvedic traditions. Ghee can be found in most grocery stores and online, but you can also make it yourself by cooking butter in a saucepan on low heat until the solids turn brown. Strain through cheesecloth to separate the milk solids. The ghee can be stored in an airtight container at room temperature or refrigerated.

Haddock: Native to the North Atlantic, haddock are part of the cod family of fish. They can be substituted with cod, Pacific rockfish, halibut, or pollock.

Kefir: A fermented milk drink, with a flavour like yoghurt or buttermilk. For the purposes of this book, it can be substituted with buttermilk or plain yoghurt thinned out with a bit of milk or water until it is a pourable consistency.

Mace: This spice is actually made from the outer coating of the nutmeg seed. As such, it has a similar flavour profile to nutmeg but is milder, with a sweet, woody fragrance. It can be found in the spice section of most grocery stores and online.

Masa harina: Made from nixtamalised corn (that is, corn treated with slaked lime) which has been ground into a fine flour. Although most commonly used to make corn tortillas, tamales, and pupusas, it can also be used as a thickener for soups, stews, and chilli, lending the final product a hint of corn flavour. It can be found in most grocery stores, Latin American markets, and online.

Mexican crema: Similar to sour cream, Mexican crema is richer, creamier, and tangier. It can be found in many grocery stores and Latin American markets. If you can't find it readily, you can make a substitute by combining sour cream with enough double/heavy cream to make it a thick but pourable consistency and lime juice to taste for a bit of tang.

Mortadella: This is an emulsified pork sausage originating from Italy. In addition to pork, it typically contains pistachios, black peppercorns, and myrtle berries. It has a silky mouthfeel and a rich pork flavour with slightly nutty, peppery notes and a hint of spice. It can be found in supermarkets, either prepackaged or fresh-cut from the deli counter.

Octopus: This can be found in the seafood section of many grocery stores, typically fresh or frozen, but can also be found in fish markets, speciality markets, and even online retailers. Some markets will even sell just the tentacles, precooked. If you can find precooked tentacles, you can save some time with the Karambwan (page 16) and skip right to the grilling process.

Orange blossom water: Created during the distillation of bitter orange blossoms to make essential oil, this flavoured water has a bright, citrusy, floral flavour. It is used in cuisines across the world and can be found in the baking aisle of most grocery stores or online. It is also used in cocktails and may be found in the liquor aisle of some grocery stores, or in liquor stores.

Palm sugar: This natural sweetener is used in Southeast Asian cuisines and is derived from palm sap. It has a slightly smoky, rich caramel flavour and can be found in baking aisles of some grocery stores, Asian markets, and online.

Petal powder and lustre dust: These are edible, powdered food colourings, typically used to add vibrant colour to baked goods, either in the batter or dough, or as components of the decoration. They can be found in some craft stores, speciality baking supply shops, and online.

DIETARY CONSIDERATIONS

Recipe	Page	Gluten-Free	Nondairy	Vegan	Vegetarian
Anchovy Pizza	119				
Arc Gumbo	29		X		
Asgarnian Ale	126		X	X	X
Baked Potato	41	X			X
Batta	115				X
Blurberry Special	125	X	X	X	X
Brûlée Supreme	88	X			X
Cabbage Garden Pie	44				X
Cake, Four Ways	93				X
Cheesecake	96				X
Chocchip Crunchies	105				X
Chilli con Carne	30	X			
Chilli Potato	41	X			
Chocolate Saturday	131	X			
Cooked Fishcake	13		X		
Cooked Jubbly	67	X	X		
Cooked Meat	68	X			
Cooked Oomlie Wrap	56	X			
Curry	82				
Dwarven Rock Cake	100				
Egg Potato	41	X			
Festive Gingerbread Cookies	103				
Fish	59	X	X		
Fried Mushrooms	51				
Fried Onions	17				
Gianne Dough	112		X	X	
Gnomebowls	121		X	X	
Goulash	31				

Recipe	Page	Gluten-Free	Nondairy	Vegan	Vegetarian
Green Gloop Soup	26	X			
Holy Biscuits	106				X
Infernal Sauce	36	X	X	X	X
Karambwan	16	X			
Karamjan Rum with Sliced Bananas	99	X			X
Lobster	63	X	X		
Mature Cider	129	X	X	X	X
Meat Pizza	119				
Pineapple Pizza	119				X
Pitta Bread	113		X	X	X
Poison Chalice	128	X			X
Pumpkin	48				
Purple Sweets	109	X			X
Red Hot Sauce	34	X	X	X	X
Redberry Pie	97				X
Roast Beast Meat	72				
Rocktail Soup	25	X			
Short Green Guy	132	X	X	X	X
Shrimps	60	X			
Slop of Compromise	87				X
Spicy Sauce	35	X	X	X	X
Spider on Stick	14		X		
Spinach Roll	19				X
Stew	24	X			
Stuffed Snake	63				
Terrible Pie	75				
Tuna and Corn	79	X			
Tuna Potato	41	X			
Ugthanki Kebab	5				
Veggie Mush	47	X			X
Wild Pie	71				
Yellow Spicy Stew	23				

DIFFICULTY INDEX

ABOUT THE AUTHORS

JARRETT MELENDEZ grew up on the mean, deer-infested streets of Bucksport, Maine. A former chef and line cook, Jarrett has worked in restaurants, diners, and bakeries throughout New England and Mexico and got instruction on Japanese home cooking from some very patient host mothers when he lived in Tokyo and Hiroshima. He's been a professional writer since 2009 but started working as a recipe developer and food writer in 2020. His work has appeared on *Bon Appétit*, *Saveur*, *Epicurious*, and *Food52*, and he is the author of *The Comic Kitchen*, an upcoming fully illustrated, comic-style cookbook. When not cooking and writing about food, Jarrett is also an award-winning comic book writer. His best-known work is *Chef's Kiss* from Oni Press, which won the Alex Award from the American Library Association and a GLAAD award nomination for Outstanding Graphic Novel, in addition to being nominated for an Eisner Award for Best Publication for Teens. Jarrett has contributed to the Ringo-nominated *All We Ever Wanted*, *Full Bleed*, *Young Men in Love*, and *Murder Hobo: Chaotic Neutral*. He is currently working on *Tales of the Fungo: The Legend of Cep*, a middle-grade fantasy adventure, to be published by Andrews McMeel. He lives in Massachusetts with his collection of Monokuro Boo plush pigs.

SANDRA ROSNER wanders the shattered ruins, distant wilds, and frozen wastes in search of lore and stories that capture the imagination. She is an author and novelist of fantasy, sci-fi, and historical genres and has contributed to a number of published works as a developmental editor. When not crafting worlds of her own, Sandra enjoys TTRPGs, leading raids online, and exploring the old growth of the Pacific Northwest.

MEASUREMENT CONVERSION CHART

VOLUMES

US	METRIC
⅕ teaspoon	1 ml
1 teaspoon	5 ml
1 tablespoon	15 ml
1 fluid ounce	30 ml
⅕ cup	50 ml
¼ cup	60 ml
⅓ cup	80 ml
3.4 fluid ounces	100 ml
½ cup	120 ml
⅔ cup	160 ml
¾ cup	180 ml
1 cup	240 ml
1 pint (2 cups)	480 ml
1 quart (4 cups)	.95 liter

TEMPERATURES

FAHRENHEIT	CELSIUS
200°	93.3°
212°	100°
250°	120°
275°	135°
300°	150°
325°	165°
350°	177°
400°	205°
425°	220°
450°	233°
475°	245°
500°	260°

WEIGHT

US	METRIC
0.5 ounce	14 grams
1 ounce	28 gram
¼ pound	113 grams
⅓ pound	151 grams
½ pound	227 grams
1 pound	454 grams

Published by Titan Books, London, in 2024.

TITAN
BOOKS

A division of Titan Publishing Group Ltd
144 Southwark Street
London SE1 0UP
www.titanbooks.com

Find us on Facebook: www.facebook.com/TitanBooks

Follow us on X: @titanbooks

JAGEX   RUNESCAPE | OFFICIAL RUNESCAPE® PRODUCT
© JAGEX LTD, 2023

Published by Insight Editions under license from Jagex Ltd. © Jagex Ltd. JAGEX ®, the "X" logo, RuneScape ® and Old School RuneScape ® are registered and/or unregistered trade marks of Jagex Ltd in the United Kingdom, European Union, United States and other countries.

INSIGHT
EDITIONS

Published by arrangement with Insight Editions, San Rafael, California, in 2024.
www.insighteditions.com

A CIP catalogue record for this title is available from the British Library.

ISBN: 9781803369945

Publisher: Raoul Goff
VP, Co-Publisher: Vanessa Lopez
VP, Creative: Chrissy Kwasnik
VP, Manufacturing: Alix Nicholaeff
VP, Group Managing Editor: Vicki Jaeger
Publishing Director: Mike Degler
Art Director: Catherine San Juan
Designer: Lola Villanueva
Associate Editor: Sadie Lowry
Editorial Assistant: Alex Figueiredo
Managing Editor: Maria Spano
Senior Production Editor: Nora Milman
Production Associate: Deena Hashem
Senior Production Manager, Subsidiary Rights: Lina s Palma-Temena

Text by Jarrett Melendez and Sandra Rosner
Photographer: Ted Thomas
Food and Prop Stylist: Elena P. Craig
Food Styling Assistant: Patricia C. Parrish

ROOTS of PEACE   REPLANTED PAPER

Insight Editions, in association with Roots of Peace, will plant two trees for each tree used in the manufacturing of this book. Roots of Peace is an internationally renowned humanitarian organization dedicated to eradicating land mines worldwide and converting war-torn lands into productive farms.

Manufactured in China by Insight Editions
10 9 8 7 6 5 4 3